Date: 01/25/12

J 636.7 BOL
Bolan, Sandra.
Caring for your mutt /

Caring for Your Mutt

Our Best Friends

OUR BEST FRIENDS

Caring for Your Mutt

Sandra Bolan

ELDORADO INK

Produced by OTTN Publishing, Stockton, New Jersey

Eldorado Ink
PO Box 100097
Pittsburgh, PA 15233
www.eldoradoink.com

3 5 7 9 8 6 4 2

Library of Congress Cataloging-in-Publication Data

Bolan, Sandra.
    Caring for your mutt / Sandra Bolan.
        p. cm. — (Our best friends)
    Includes bibliographical references.
    ISBN-13: 978-1-932904-20-8 (hc)
    ISBN-13: 1-932904-44-4 (trade edition)
    1. Mutts (Dogs) I. Title.
    SF427.B58 2008
    636.7—dc22

                                    2007051607

Photo credits: © American Animal Hospital Association: 32; © iStockphoto.com/Dan
Brandenburg: 25; © iStockphoto.com/Peter Dean: 116; © iStockphoto.com/David H. Lewis:
50; © iStockphoto.com/Leslie Morris: 99; © iStockphoto.com/Annette Wiechmann: 115; ©
Joel Mills: 58; used under license from Shutterstock, Inc.: 3, 8, 11, 12, 14, 15, 17, 20, 21,
23, 28, 29, 33, 34, 36, 37, 39, 41, 43, 44, 46, 47, 49, 52, 55, 56, 58, 60, 61, 66, 67, 68, 70,
72, 74, 75, 76, 79, 80, 82, 84, 86, 88, 89, 91, 93, 94, 95, 97, 98, 101, 104, 105, 108, 110,
113, 117, 118; courtesy Linda Simmons, p. 102.

TABLE OF CONTENTS

Introduction

GARY KORSGAARD, DVM

The mutually beneficial relationship between humans and animals began long before the dawn of recorded history. Archaeologists believe that humans began to capture and tame wild goats, sheep, and pigs more than 9,000 years ago. These animals were then bred for specific purposes, such as providing humans with a reliable source of food or providing furs and hides that could be used for clothing or the construction of dwellings.

Other animals had been sought for companionship and assistance even earlier. The dog, believed to be the first animal domesticated, began living and working with Stone Age humans in Europe more than 14,000 years ago. Some archaeologists believe that wild dogs and humans were drawn together because both hunted the same prey. By taming and training dogs, humans became more effective hunters. Dogs, meanwhile, enjoyed the social contact with humans and benefited from greater access to food and warm shelter. Dogs soon became beloved pets as well as trusted workers. This can be seen from the many artifacts depicting dogs that have been found at ancient sites in Asia, Europe, North America, and the Middle East.

The earliest domestic cats appeared in the Middle East about 5,000 years ago. Small wild cats were probably first attracted to human settlements because plenty of rodents could be found wherever harvested grain was stored. Cats played a useful role in hunting and killing these pests, and it is likely that grateful humans rewarded them for this assistance. Over time, these small cats gave up some of their aggressive wild behaviors and began living among humans. Cats eventually became so popular in ancient Egypt that they were believed to possess magical powers. Cat statues were placed outside homes to ward off evil spirits, and mummified cats were included in royal tombs to accompany their owners into the afterlife.

Today, few people believe that cats have supernatural powers, but most pet owners feel a magical bond with their pets, whether they are dogs, cats, hamsters, rabbits, horses, or parrots. The lives of pets and their people become inextricably inter-twined, providing strong emotional and physical rewards for both humans and animals. People of all ages can benefit from the loving com-panionship of a pet. Not surprisingly, then, pet ownership is widespread. Recent statistics indicate that about 60 percent of all households in the United States and Canada have at least one pet, while the figure is close to 50 percent of households in the United Kingdom. For millions of peo-ple, therefore, pets truly have become their "best friends."

Finding the best animal friend can be a challenge, however. Not only are there many types of domesticated pets, but each has specific needs, characteristics, and personality traits. Even within a category of pets, such as dogs, different breeds will flourish in different surroundings and with different treatment. For example, a German Shepherd may not be the right pet for a person living in a cramped urban apartment; that per-son might be better off caring for a smaller dog like a Toy Poodle or Shih Tzu, or perhaps a cat. On the other hand, an active person who loves the outdoors may prefer the companion-ship of a Labrador Retriever to that of a small dog or a passive indoor pet like a goldfish or hamster.

The joys of pet ownership come with certain responsibilities. Bringing a pet into your home and your neigh-borhood obligates you to care for and train the pet properly. For exam-ple, a dog must be housebroken, taught to obey your commands, and trained to behave appropriately when he encounters other people or ani-mals. Owners must also be mindful of their pet's particular nutritional and medical needs.

The purpose of the OUR BEST FRIENDS series is to provide a helpful and comprehensive introduction to pet ownership. Each book contains the basic information a prospective pet owner needs in order to choose the right pet for his or her situation and to care for that pet throughout the pet's lifetime. Training, socializa-tion, proper nutrition, potential medical issues, and the legal respon-sibilities of pet ownership are thoroughly explained and discussed, and an abundance of expert tips and suggestions are offered. Whether it is a hamster, corn snake, guinea pig, or Labrador Retriever, the books in the OUR BEST FRIENDS series provide everything the reader needs to know about how to have a happy, well-adjusted, and well-behaved pet.

> Most dogs are mutts, or mixed breeds—dogs of uncertain ancestry, whose forebears included canines of more than one breed. Many people believe strongly that their mixed-breed dogs make better pets than more expensive purebreds.

CHAPTER ONE

What Type of Mixed Breed Is Right for You?

Mutt, *mixed breed*, and *mongrel* are all terms commonly used to describe dogs that are the offspring of two different breeds that have randomly mated. For the most part, it's impossible to pinpoint the precise provenance of these beloved pets. Some mixed breeds clearly exhibit attributes of their parents, such as head shape, physique, or the texture of their fur. However, each dog is a jumbled-up mixture that consists of a little bit of Mom, a little bit of Dad, and a bit of their parents' parents. No two mixed breeds, even if they're from the same litter, will look or perhaps even act alike.

That's the most wonderful thing about mixed breeds—no two are identical. However, this uniqueness can pose a challenge for people who choose a mixed-breed puppy, because they can never know for certain what they will get until the puppy is older. For all they know, the puppy they hoped would grow into a strapping 50-pound (23 kilogram) bundle of athletic fun may turn out to be a smallish, lazy lapdog.

Determining the final size of a mixed breed becomes an even more challenging guessing game when two vastly different breeds mate, because you won't know, until it's too late, which side of the family the puppy will resemble. There is, however, one thing you can look at that may give you some idea of a puppy's final

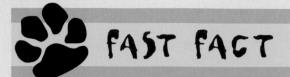

size—his paws. Generally speaking, the larger a puppy's paws, the bigger he'll be when he's full grown.

While there are 157 different breeds of dogs registered with the American Kennel Club (AKC), a handful of breeds most commonly appear in the mixed-breed population. These include the Labrador Retriever, the German Shepherd, the Golden Retriever, and the Beagle. This should come as no surprise, though, as these four breeds are typically among the five most popular dog breeds registered by the American Kennel Club.

DOG CATEGORIES

There are seven categories of dogs: sporting, hound, terrier, toy, working, herding, and non-sporting. Understanding the different categories may help you figure out which group—or groups—your mutt belongs in, and can give you some insight into his adult personality and full-grown size.

SPORTING: Dogs in this category, like Retrievers, Pointers, Spaniels, and Setters, were bred for hunting. They love to work alongside their human companions and are often happy, exuberant, and eager to please. Because working hard is in their DNA, these dogs are athletic and must be kept busy or they will make their own entertainment— which might including chewing your shoes or destroying your furniture!

There are many differences in temperament among dogs in the sporting category. For example, Pointers are particularly strong-minded and independent, which can be difficult for a novice dog owner to handle. On the other hand, Setters are typically described as soft-spirited, and their activity level can range from vigorous (Irish Setter) to calm (English Setter). The variety

within this one category of dogs exemplifies the vast variations possible when dogs start randomly mating.

HOUNDS: This group includes dogs like the Afghan, the Beagle, the Bloodhound, the Greyhound, and the Whippet. They were originally bred for tracking, either by scent or by sight. Nowadays, most people don't use these dogs for hunting, so their keen senses and instincts can get them into trouble. Hounds, whether they hunt by sight or scent, should never be let off-leash in an unfenced area as their eyes and noses will quickly lead them astray.

Sight hounds, such as the Afghan and the Greyhound, are the couch potatoes of the group, but once a moving object catches their attention, they have the ability to pursue it until it's captured. Scent hounds like the Beagle or the Bloodhound, on the other hand, have been described as single-minded, nose-to-the-ground dogs that are always busy sniffing something. When left alone, bored, or excited, scent hounds become barkers. Historically, their strong, loud bays scared prey and

Sporting dogs will always be up for a fun game of "fetch" with their humans.

alerted their owners as to their whereabouts.

TERRIERS: Typically, terriers are small but fearless and strong-willed dogs. These dogs will fight back when attacked, even if the opponent is two to three times their size. Terriers must be socialized to accept unfamiliar people and animals. Otherwise, some of them become aggressive and predatory. Miniature Schnauzers, West Highland Terriers, and Cairn Terriers are the most popular dogs in this group.

Terriers were originally bred to hunt and kill vermin, such as rats and foxes. However, some smaller terrier breeds were bred down from larger terriers for use as companion dogs, rather than as hunters. These dogs are typically included in the next category, toy dogs.

TOY: Dogs in this category were bred for one reason only—to keep people company. Toy dog breeds include the Pomeranian, the Chihuahua, the Yorkshire Terrier, and the Toy Poodle. While popular with the elderly and those who live in apartments, toy dogs can be demanding and bossy. These small dogs can also be difficult to live with when their owners fail to properly socialize and train them.

Common problems with these breeds include excessive barking, picky eating, and refusing to walk on a leash. Owners who treat these dogs like stuffed animals rather than dogs often cause these problems themselves. Many of these owners refuse to take their pets to obedience training, wrongly believing that their dog is so small that he can't do much damage. A bored dog, no matter how

Smaller dog breeds are popular among young people who want a friend that is easily portable.

FAMOUS MIXED BREEDS

Some relatively famous dogs have been mixed breeds. For example, Velvet, who saved three climbers on Oregon's Mount Hood in 2007, is a Lab/Cattle Dog mix. Lava, the canine star of *From Baghdad, With Love*, is a dog of unknown origin. Maui, who played Murray on the television show *Mad About You*, is a Border Collie mix. Higgins, who played Benji in several popular movies during the 1970s, was a Poodle/Schnauzer/Cocker Spaniel mix.

And Spike from the movie *Old Yeller* was a Lab mix.

Numerous famous people have also adopted mixed breeds. Actress Alicia Silverstone owns a Pit Bull/Doberman/Rottweiler mix, named Samson. Ashley Judd owns two Cockapoos, named Buttermilk and Shag. Drew Barrymore owns two Lab/Chow mixes, named Flossie and Templeton. And Matthew McConaughey has a Lab/Chow mix he named Miss Hud.

diminutive his size, can still tear apart a couch with relative ease.

WORKING: The working dog was bred to take on a variety of tasks alongside his human companion. Dogs within this group can be broken down into flock guarders, gentle giants, and the Nordic breeds.

Flock guard dogs, which include the Anatolian Shepherd, the Great Pyrenees, the Komondor, and the Kuvasze, are not for the novice dog owner because they are naturally suspicious and independent thinkers. These dogs need a lot of training, and it must be made clear to them who's in charge of the household. Constant socialization with other dogs and animals is also required.

The guard dogs in this group include the Akita, the Doberman, the Giant Schnauzer, the Great Dane, and the Rottweiler. While breeding has softened the rough edges of these dogs somewhat, they can still be a challenge to live with because of their strong drive, focus, and commitment. These are dogs that must be kept busy or they'll make up their own destructive to-do list, chewing walls and eating furniture. At the same time, these dogs must be trained in a positive way, as these breeds will respond to aggression with aggression.

Gentle giants, another subgroup of the working dog category, includes the Bernese Mountain Dog, the Newfoundland, and the Saint

Large dogs like this Newfoundland have a gentle, easygoing nature, but they require a great deal of training and care if they are to live in a family with small children.

Bernard. All these dogs are easygoing, lovable, and slobbery. Again, however, training from a young age is an absolute must, simply because of their size. In addition, many of these dogs shed a great deal, so prospective owners should be aware of the amount of care that will be required in cleaning up after them.

The Nordic dogs, such as the Alaskan Malamute, the Samoyed, and the Siberian Husky, were originally bred to survive the harsh, frigid northern climate, where they were used to pull sleds, herd, hunt, and

guard. These dogs are physically and mentally tough and are often described as being strong-willed and active, yet very fun-loving. Like the gentle giants, these dogs shed a lot all year long, but in particular during the fall and spring seasons when they are losing the previous season's coat.

HERDING: Herding dogs once belonged to the working dog group, but in 1983 the American Kennel Club gave them a category all their own. Herding dogs were bred to control the movement of other animals, such as cattle or sheep on a farm. This trait is deeply ingrained in their DNA, so a herding dog that's a companion animal will still find something to herd, whether it's children or other animals in the house. Because these dogs were bred to work, they have a lot of energy and may drive their owners crazy if they don't get enough exercise. With their intelligence, natural athletic abilities, and fine work ethic, these dogs excel in sporting activities like Agility and Flyball.

Herders cannot be left home alone all day long or they will methodically tear up the house. Common herding dogs include the German Shepherd, the Border Collie, the Australian Shepherd, and the Welsh Corgi.

NON-SPORTING: This group, a catch-all category for the AKC, includes a wide variety of dogs, such as the Boston Terrier, the Bulldog, the American Eskimo Dog, and the Bichon Frise. The only thing these

Dogs in the herding category were bred to help take care of goats, sheep, and other animals.

dogs really have in common is that they are no longer generally being bred or used for their original purpose.

By understanding the characteristics of the seven groups of purebred dogs, you will have a better idea of what your mixed-breed dog's temperament and size may be. But these traits are only generalizations. Each dog, whether he's a purebred or a mixed breed, has his own unique personality.

DIFFERENCES BETWEEN PUREBREDS AND MIXED BREEDS

Is there really a difference between purebred and mixed-breed dogs? Yes, there are quite a few differences that range from the actual price of the dog to what you can do with him competitively.

For one thing, a purebred dog comes with registration papers and a chart detailing his family tree, which is probably littered with

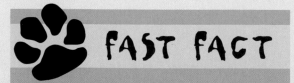

FAST FACT

Dogs descended from many generations of mixed breeds tend to be light brown or black in coloring, mid-sized, and about 40 pounds (18 kg) with a pointed nose and upright ears.

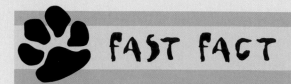

FAST FACT

No matter what their size or breed, all dogs have 321 bones and 42 permanent teeth.

Conformation show and/or Obedience competition champions. On the other hand, a mixed-breed dog comes with no detailed family tree—if he did, it would have so many branches it would look more like a forest than a tree. There is little chance of finding a Conformation champion in a mixed-breed's bloodline.

Second, a purebred's size, coloring, health, and temperament are known entities, as these dogs have been homogenized through years of selective breeding. A mixed breed, however, is a jumble of various large and small dogs. Some may have had long, flowing fur; others had short, course coats. Some were well-tempered, while others were snappy and vicious. The litter was most likely the result of a chance encounter between two dogs, not a carefully planned coupling, as happens with purebreds. Therefore, the mixed-breed litter produced may not be the healthiest. Unless you find him as an adult, a mixed breed's temperament and health history will be complete mysteries.

Mixed breeds are, unfortunately, often rescued from unfavorable circumstances or have never known life in a human family. This means the dog that captures your heart may be unsociable and afraid of strangers. This is something that can potentially be overcome, but it takes a lot of time and patience. Purebreds, on the other hand, are often bred by reputable breeders who try to ensure that puppies don't have undesirable characteristics.

CROSSBREEDS

While mixed breeds, for the most part, are the by-products of accidental matings, there are some people who have purposely bred two different purebred dogs together with the intention of producing dogs that have the best characteristics of both breeds. Examples of these crossbreeds are the Labradoodle, a Labrador Retriever crossed with a Poodle; the Goldendoodle, a Golden Retriever crossed with a Poodle; the Dorgi, a Corgi crossed with a Dashhound; a Puggle, a Pug crossed with a Beagle; and a Borderjack, a Border Collie crossed with a Jack Russell Terrier.

One advantage to owning a crossbreed as opposed to a mixed-breed dog is that you can be fairly certain of the dog's temperament and size because you know the parental characteristics. That doesn't mean you'll get a cookie-cutter dog, though. For example, a Labradoodle litter can contain puppies that have a Lab's coarse, short, double coat, a tightly curled Poodle coat, or a shaggy mix of the two.

There are thousands of possible combinations for crossbred dogs, each with its own particular charm. This pleasant fellow, for example, is a cross between a Beagle and a Rottweiler.

POPULAR CROSSBREEDS

The Poodle has become one of the most popular breeds in North America over the past few years, thanks in part to claims that these dogs are hypoallergenic. For this reason, a number of Poodle mixes have also become very popular. These include the following:

- Labradoodle (Labrador Retriever and Poodle)
- Goldendoodle (Golden Retriever and Poodle)
- Cockapoo (Cocker Spaniel and Poodle)
- Peekapoo (Pekingese and Poodle)
- Schnoodle (Schnauzer and Poodle)
- Yorkipoo (Yorkshire Terrier and Poodle)
- Maltipoo (Maltese and Poodle)

Poodle mixes, for the most part, do shed much less than the average dog, but the claim that they are allergen-free is not quite true. People who are allergic to dogs are more likely to be allergic to a dog's saliva than to the dog's dander (dry, dead skin cells) or fur. Therefore, even a supposedly hypoallergenic dog can still provoke an allergic reaction in people who are very sensitive.

When it comes to crossbreeds, a first-generation crossbreed is a dog that is the by-product of two purebred dogs. First-generation crossbreeds may or may not have undesirable attributes, and they will probably look more like one parent than the other. On the upside, because these dogs are presumably bred from healthy purebred dogs, the chances of the offspring suffering from hereditary diseases are minimized.

A generational crossbreed is one that is the offspring of two first-generation crossbreeds. Generational dogs may be the only mixed-breed dogs that are relatively consistent in looks and personality. However, there is always the possibility of a recessive gene coming to the fore and producing an unexpected trait. Generational crossbreeds are also more apt to suffer from diseases that are not apparent in first-generation crossbreeds.

When searching for crossbreeds, you may find them described as designer dogs or even rare dogs. You

FAST FACT

The American Kennel Club, the Canadian Kennel Club, and the Kennel Club of the United Kingdom do not recognize or register crossbreeds, because mating two purebreds does not create a new breed.

may even find that they come with a hefty price tag—a crossbreed might even cost twice the price of a purebred dog from a reputable breeder. However, crossbreeds are not rare, and should not cost thousands of dollars. Being labeled "rare" or "designer" is a clever marketing tactic used by some unscrupulous breeders to make money. Dogs with the same or very similar lineage can often to be found at the local pound for a fraction of the cost.

THE BEST MUTT FOR YOU

Now that you know what the purebred components of a mixed breed are, it's time for you to determine which type of mixed-breed dog is best for you. In deciding what type of mixed breed you want, first and foremost you have to consider your lifestyle. Are you an active person who likes hiking and participating in outdoor pursuits that a dog would

enjoy alongside you? If so, then a medium-sized dog with some retriever or other sporting dog in him is a good choice, as are mixed breeds with some working or herding lineage.

On the other hand, if you're something of a couch potato looking for a dog to sit beside you while you're watching television, then you may want to consider a mixed breed with some hound in him. These dogs are typically happy to do nothing, unless something triggers their sense of smell or sight. Hounds can be stubbornly single-minded about following interesting smells or sights until their instincts have been satisfied.

How about your family? Do they want a dog? Do you have children who are old enough to take on some of the simple tasks involved in owning a dog, such as feeding or walking him, providing the dog is small enough? Or are the children so young that a dog may complicate an already hectic household situation? All family members must agree with the decision to bring a dog into the home, because caring for a dog, no matter what the breed, is a family affair.

If you have young children, you need to carefully consider the size of the dog you want. A toy mix may not be suitable because these dogs are generally not hearty enough to withstand the roughhousing and ear and tail pulling common when children encounter dogs. On the flip side, you may want to stay away from the very large dogs, because one wag of the tail can potentially knock a small child down. These dogs are not ones you want to invite to teatime, let alone try to dress up.

Prospective dog owners should also consider their living situation. Do you live in a house with a large, fenced-in yard, or are you in an apartment building, co-op, or a condo complex? If you live in an apartment or other multifamily dwelling, are dogs allowed and is there a size restriction? If you live in an apartment that allows dogs, are there parks nearby where you can go with your dog for some fresh air and exercise? These may seem like picky details that can be dealt with once the dog is home, but bringing a dog into an unsuitable environment is the most common reason that dogs are surrendered to shelters.

THE PRICE OF OWNING A DOG

The cost of owning a dog, whether he's a purebred or a mixed breed,

Your current living situation and the makeup of your family must be considered when you are deciding what kind of dog you want.

Food and supplies for your dog, such as leashes, food bowls, chew toys, bedding, and other items, will probably cost several hundred dollars in the first year.

varies based on a number of factors, such as overall health and age. During a dog's first year, you'll spend at least $850 on his care, and that doesn't include the actual price of the dog. When it comes to the cost of purchasing a dog, a mixed breed is definitely cheaper than a purebred; many shelters and rescue groups charge a nominal fee that can be as low as $20. Sometimes friends have puppies that they are willing to give away to a good home for free. On the other hand, a purebred often costs hundreds of dollars.

The typical post-purchase cost of dog ownership breaks down like this:

ROUTINE VETERINARY CARE: $100 to $500. The price varies because it depends on how much your veterinarian charges for examinations and which tests are conducted.

NON-ROUTINE VETERINARY CARE: It's a good idea to a have slush fund available for this kind of non-routine care, just in case, as accidents are bound to happen. The price will vary depending on how many emergency visits you have to make.

FOOD AND TREATS: $150 to $500. There is a broad price range because the cost of food greatly depends on the size of the dog and the quality of food you feed him. A premium-brand food will cost more, but your dog will be healthier overall and will be less likely to require medical attention. (This will be discussed in greater depth on pages 70–71.) Treats should also be of a very high quality.

ANNUAL PARASITE TREATMENT AND CONTROL: $100 to $150.

IMMUNIZATION: $50 to $100. This is something that must be budgeted for on an annual basis.

SPAY OR NEUTER: $50 to $200. This is a one-time fee, which depends on what your vet charges. However, if you got your mixed breed from a shelter or rescue group, this procedure will probably have already been performed. If not, the shelter may offer to have this operation done at a discounted rate. Some shelters will not allow dogs to be adopted unless they've been spayed or neutered.

MISCELLANEOUS EXPENSES: $300 to $2,000. This includes a crate and baby gates, both of which are an absolute must when it comes to housetraining any dog, as well as toys, leashes, food and water bowls, and other assorted items.

OBEDIENCE SCHOOL: $100 to $500. If your mixed breed is a bit older and is already trained, then you won't need to attend obedience classes. However, if you're interested in doing something with your dog to help build your bond with each other, then this is a great activity.

You don't need to spend a fortune on obedience training, but you must choose a school that's right for you. Most training classes cost $100 to $300 for a program that lasts for several weeks. Another option is private training, which often costs about $50 an hour. If you decide to participate in a specialized activity with your dog, the cost of training will increase still further.

CHAPTER TWO

Finding the Perfect Mutt

You need to be just as selective in deciding where to get your mixed-breed dog as you are in choosing him. The first place to look for your mixed breed is at your local animal shelter. That's where you'll find dogs brought in by their owners for a variety of reasons, including the most popular one: "My children are allergic to him." Among other common reasons for dogs being surrendered to shelters are the following: the family is moving to a place that doesn't allow dogs; the owners are getting divorced; the owners are having a baby; or the owner got a new job that no longer allows him to care for the dog properly.

Many great dogs—both purebreds and mixed-breeds—can be found at the local pound.

All these are owner-related issues, which are not a reflection on the behavior of the dog. In these cases the dog just got caught in the middle of a lifestyle change, and the owners thought it best to let someone else take over caring for the animal.

Make no mistake, some dogs in shelters do have behavioral issues. However, it can be argued that most canine behavioral issues are owner-related. Nine times out of ten, when a dog with behavioral issues ends up at a shelter, it's because the owners got in over their heads. They may have brought a cute little puppy home, not realizing that he would grow to 80 pounds (36 kg) in nine months and require regular runs in the park in order to burn off his abundant energy. Sometimes, owners don't understand that dogs need to be taught not to urinate in the house, bite people's ankles, or growl at strangers. Instead of learning how to correct these behaviors, or how to prevent them in the first place, the owner labels the dog problematic

and dumps him at the shelter. Many of these dogs can make great companions for people willing to invest the time and effort required to properly train and care for them.

Another place to look for dogs is through all-breed rescue organizations. Rescue groups differ from shelters in that these groups typically have a network of foster homes where rescued dogs live while they're awaiting adoption. Dogs in shelters live in cages inside a clean, but not very homey, building alongside a multitude of other dogs. In the rescue group's foster home, the rescuing family can do real-life evaluations so they know if the dog barks when the doorbell rings, whether or not he gets along with children or other animals, if he's fearful of thunderstorms, or if he likes to dig up the backyard.

Foster parents can also work one-on-one with dogs that have behavioral problems in order to make them adoptable. Shelters are rarely able to do in-depth evaluations—typically, there are too many dogs and not enough staff members. Shelter workers also don't know what the dog is really like in the home environment, as all they know is what the person who dropped him off has told them, and that information may or may not be true.

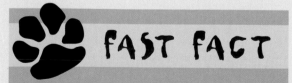

FAST FACT

People who own pets traditionally live longer, are less stressed, and have fewer heart attacks.

ADOPTING A DOG FROM A SHELTER OR RESCUE GROUP

Adopting from a shelter or rescue group is not as simple as walking into the shelter, picking a dog, and going home with him. The adoption process can be a lengthy one, depending on the number of available dogs, your compatibility with them, and the number of people on a waiting list for the kind of dog you want. Like a breeder, the adoption agency will question you about your lifestyle and your reasons for wanting a dog. Adoption counselors will also ask you about your housing situa-tion. Do you rent a house or apart-ment, or own your own home? Do you have a fenced-in backyard? After all, this is at least the second home where this dog will be taking up resi-dence, and these organizations want to make sure this is the last home he will ever have.

You will also be required to complete an adoption application and provide references. If you owned a dog previously, it would be a good idea to include positive references from your veterinarian and, if applicable, a dog trainer with whom you have worked.

The volunteers at breed rescue organizations are typically very knowledgeable about dogs and their care, and can be a great resource for the first-time dog owner.

A part of the screening process may also include a home visit before adoption. This is to ensure that your home is indeed suitable for the dog you want to adopt. Another home visit may occur sometime after the adoption. The second visit is designed to make sure that the transition for you and your new canine companion is going well.

At times, more than one family will be interested in the same dog. The staff at the shelter or rescue organization will make the final decision as to who gets each dog, based on what they observe during the screening process.

OTHER SOURCES OF MIXED BREEDS

Another place to look for mixed breeds is on the Internet. There are numerous rescue organizations across North America that post photos of their available dogs online to broaden the scope of prospective "forever homes." By searching online, you have a better chance of finding the type of mixed breed you're looking for, especially if you have specific requirements.

If you find the perfect dog online, there's a very good chance that he may be living across the country, so meeting your new dog before adopting him may be a challenge. If you

find yourself in this situation, make sure that you spend a lot of time talking to the foster family or shelter workers about the dog's temperament, previous situation, health, and behavioral issues that you may have to contend with. It would be unfair, not to mention terribly traumatic, for you to bring a dog across the country only to drop him off at another shelter a few weeks or a month later because you didn't make an informed adoption. In an Internet situation, you must be willing to accept and expect the unexpected.

A more local option is the newspaper. This is often where you'll find dogs that are free to a good home or available for a nominal fee. Before

You may be able to find trainers, groomers, and even puppies through the classified ads in your local newspaper.

deciding to adopt a dog advertised in the newspaper, ask yourself why the dog is really up for adoption. Again, chances are it's because the owners didn't do their research and brought a dog into their home that they really weren't equipped to raise.

Go to the owner's home to look at the dog. While there, pay attention to his living conditions. Does it look like the dog was a part of the family or was he relegated to the backyard or the garage most of the time? Are there children around? How do they treat the dog? Also pay attention to how the owner interacts with the dog when introducing him to you. If she's aggressively yanking on the dog's collar and yelling while the dog is trying to happily greet you, then it's quite possible this person has no idea how to deal with dogs and some obedience work will be required.

Potential owners should be wary of buying from puppy mills, pet stores, and backyard breeders. All these places may charge a premium for a dog that was bred with no regard to potential health problems. These dogs typically live in small, filthy crates or enclosed areas with little human interaction, let alone playtime with other dogs. They were also probably fed a poor-quality diet.

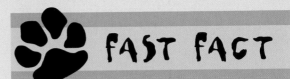

FAST FACT

More than 8 million pets are euthanatized each year due to overcrowding in animal shelters.

In general, these dogs are under-socialized and unhealthy, which can be problematic for the novice dog owner. These dogs will likely be costly to care for, as they are at risk for a litany of health issues that must be dealt with throughout their lives. These dogs may also live shorter lives for the very same reasons.

WHAT TO LOOK FOR IN A PUPPY

Once you know the type of mixed breed you want to join your family, finding a puppy is usually fairly easy. To choose the best one for you and your family, you have to look beyond their cuteness, as tough as that will be, and focus on each pup's personality.

If you're able to see the litter as a whole, watch how they interact with each other. Which puppies are pushy, outgoing, bossy, and vocal? Which ones are gentle, submissive, and quiet? Which puppies grab all the toys or win the tug-of-war games that will often spontaneously break out? And finally, pay attention to which puppies appear to be smaller

Both male and female mixed-breed dogs can make outstanding companions.

and picked on. All these types of puppies are adoptable, but only into the right home.

MALE OR FEMALE

When it comes to personality and temperament, there is a difference between the genders. One is not better than the other, just different. So you need to consider whether you want a male or a female dog.

Female dogs are typically more relaxed, though they can also be very independent and bossy. Females also have a reputation for being protective, which includes barking at every strange sound they hear. A female dog is affectionate, but only when she wants to be, not necessarily when you want her to be. Much like a cat, she will come up to you, demand to be petted, and, once she's had enough, get up and leave. If you have young children, they will provide the perfect opportunity for your female mixed breed to use her "mothering" skills. However, mood swings are also part of the female dog's temperament. She can be as sweet as pie one minute, grumpy and sulking in a corner the next. This can be somewhat minimized by having her spayed, which eliminates her heat cycles.

If you want a dog that's very affectionate and has no trouble showing it, then a male mutt is for you. Males have a relatively stable temperament, when compared to females, but all dogs have individual personalities. You may find that your female mixed breed is clingier than anticipated, while your male dog is more aloof.

Most dogs, when properly socialized, typically get along with other dogs. If you're planning on bringing a dog into a home that already has a dog, let the two dogs meet on neutral ground. If the meeting goes well, then you can proceed with the final stages of the adoption. If one acts aggressively toward the other, then it's best to continue your search.

PUPPY TESTS

There are a series of puppy tests you can easily do that will help you make a final decision. You should do these simple tests in an area away from the other puppies and with the permission of the owner. Unless you're looking for specific characteristics that will make for an exceptional canine athlete, you'd be wise to choose a dog that is neither too pushy nor too submissive. Whether male or female, a puppy that's too dominant will generally challenge other dogs and their owners for top billing in the household. You're supposed to be the dog's pack leader, so unless you're an experienced dog owner, it's best to avoid the alpha dog. On the other hand, a submissive puppy can be just as challenging to live with, as he may become a fear biter. These dogs must be carefully trained and socialized and are therefore not a good choice for the novice dog owner.

If possible, watch a litter of puppies play together. This will give you some idea of each puppy's personality.

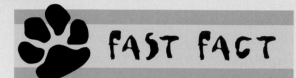

The most respected test is the Volhard Puppy Aptitude Test (PAT), which was developed by world-renowned dog specialists Jack and Wendy Volhard. The Volhard PAT assesses the following characteristics: social attraction, following, restraint, social dominance, and elevation dominance. It can be viewed at www.volhard.com/puppy/pat.htm. Scores range from one to six, with three being ideal. According to the Volhard PAT, a puppy rated three accepts and responds to human leaders easily; is the best prospect for the average owner; adapts well to new situations; is generally good with children and elderly people, although he may be inclined to be active; makes a good obedience prospect; and usually has a common-sense approach to life.

Here's how to administer the PAT:

SOCIAL ATTRACTION: You're testing the puppy's confidence and dependence. Kneel down and clap your hands to get the puppy's attention and coax him toward you. Ideally, the puppy will happily come to you with his tail up.

FOLLOWING: This tests his independence. A puppy that will not follow you is an independent, free spirit that may be difficult to train because he's more interested in the world around him than in you. You do the test by simply standing up and walking away from the puppy. But you have to make sure that he sees you walk away. Ideally, the puppy will readily follow you with his tail up.

RESTRAINT: This tells us how well the puppy accepts stress when he's physically or socially dominated. In a nutshell, you want to know if he's submissive or dominant. Gently roll the puppy onto his back and hold him there for 30 seconds. His ideal reaction will be to settle, struggle, then settle again with some eye contact.

SOCIAL DOMINANCE: With the puppy standing and you crouching beside him, pet the puppy from his head to his rump. The purpose of this test is to see if he'll try to dominate you (jump up or nip you). Both reactions indicate an independent dog. You ideally want the puppy to cuddle and lick your face.

ELEVATION DOMINANCE: Here you're testing the puppy's ability to accept being dominated in a situation over which he has absolutely no control. Cradle the puppy under his tummy, palms facing upwards and fingers clasped together. Lift the puppy off the ground a little bit. Hold him in the air for 30 seconds. He should be comfortable with you doing this.

If there's only one puppy to evaluate, you can do all the same tests, but don't be surprised if he takes a little bit of time to warm up to you. He has no doubt had very little handling, so he just may not be sure what to make of the whole situation.

ADOPTING AN OLDER DOG

Adopting an older dog has both advantages and disadvantages. One big advantage is that you know his final size and fur type, both of which are important issues for many dog owners. The best-case scenario is that you're going to be lucky enough to adopt a dog that came from a loving home, whose owners took the time to train and socialize him. With these kinds of adult dogs, the transition into a new home is often relatively easy. It will take time for the two of you to get to know each other, but any behavioral issues

shouldn't be to difficult for you to work through.

However, far too many adult dogs are in shelters because their owners tried living with an untrained puppy for six or nine months and eventually just gave up on ever having the dog tone down his exuberance or mind his manners. Again, it is the owner, not the dog, who failed in this relationship. These dogs don't have behavioral issues, per se, just bad habits that need to be unlearned. Unless trained otherwise, dogs will do whatever they want—and can get away with.

Sometimes these original owners raised their dogs in situations that promoted behavioral issues. For example, the dog might have been chained up outside all the time because the owner believed that big dogs should live outside. The result? An antisocial and aggressive dog. Depending on the mix of the dog, he may also have become extremely territorial.

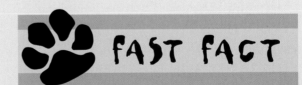

FAST FACT

There are approximately 68 million dogs owned by people in the United States, which amounts to roughly one dog per every three households.

Another common behavior in untrained dogs is counter surfing. A large dog will clear any and all counters unless he's taught that this behavior will not be tolerated. Stealing food is a common complaint from people who have not properly trained their pets. A dog may also bark excessively at strangers, which can be construed as a frightening show of aggression.

Adult dogs with behavioral problems are not dogs for the novice owner or for someone with children. A lot of training and possibly some work with a canine behaviorist will be required to retrain these types of dogs. Successful retraining will require a great deal of time and patience. However, for people who possess these gifts, adopting a dog with behavior issues and making him into a lovable animal companion can be extremely rewarding.

CHOOSING A VET

When it comes to the health care of your dog, it's important to choose a veterinarian who works well with both you and your dog. Whether you're bringing home an adult dog or a puppy, you want to take him to the vet within the first 24 hours for an introduction and an overall health check. Depending on where you got your dog, there is a greater than 50

percent chance that the dog will have some sort of health problem. It may be as basic as fleas, but any sort of health concern needs to be dealt with immediately. Therefore, be sure to choose a vet before you bring your new dog home.

Start your search for a vet by asking where your dog-owning friends, family members, and neighbors take their dogs, and ask them what they like about their

Ideally, a prospective veterinary clinic should be a member of the American Animal Hospital Association or a similar organization that inspects and accredits veterinary facilities.

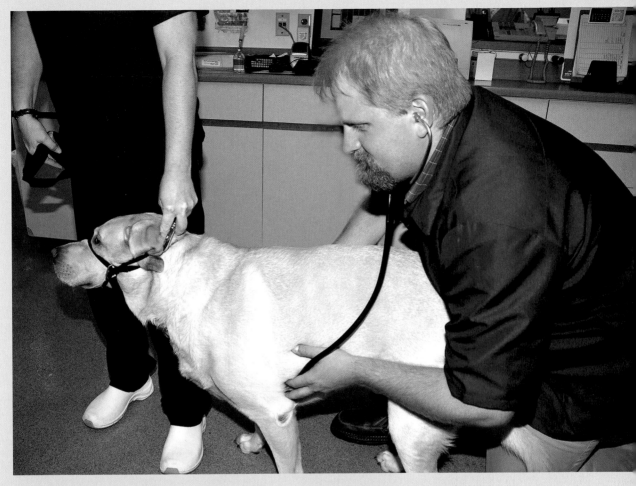

It is important to find a veterinarian that you feel comfortable with and trust. Depending on your dog's lifespan, he may be seeing this doctor for 10 years or more.

veterinary clinic. Also get recommendations from your adoption agency or area shelter, as well as the American Animal Hospital Association (AAHA). AAHA member clinics are regularly inspected and must meet specific standards established by the organization.

Ask about any emergency situations your friends may have had with their dog at the clinic. Were the staff members compassionate and caring? Did they provide updates on a regular basis?

Think about location, but don't make this your only criterion. You may find that you are more comfortable with the clinic that is 20 minutes away than the one around the corner from your home. Keep in mind, however, that in an emergency you are going to need to get your pet somewhere quickly. Veterinarians who are an hour away won't be able to help in a crisis.

Once you've narrowed down your prospects, give each one a call. Explain to the receptionist that you're about to bring home a new dog and that you need a veterinarian. Ask if they're taking on new patients, what their hours are, what services they provide, how many veterinarians are on staff, and if they specialize in any particular areas.

Be sure to ask about their fees. The cost of a regular vet visit should

not be the deciding factor, but it's something you should know up front, as the fees can vary considerably from clinic to clinic.

Not only will the initial phone interview give you some important information about the clinic, but it will also give you some sense of their customer service. If the person answering the phone is rushed and rude to you, that may be an indication of how the entire practice is run. You want the front office staff, technicians, and veterinarians to be conscientious,

When you visit a veterinary clinic, ask to see the entire facility.

thorough, and kind to you and your dog.

TAKE A TOUR OF THE CLINIC

Once you've narrowed down your choice of potential clinics to one or two, ask to take a tour. A good clinic will have no problem showing a prospective client around. When you first enter the clinic, pay attention to how you are greeted. Look around the reception area. Is it clean and tidy and are there up-to-date pet magazines? Is there a notice board with posters for lost pets or posters offering pets to good homes? Are there thank-you cards on the front counter? Those cards provide great references, because they're from pet owners testifying that they were extremely satisfied with the care their animal pals recently received.

How clean is the clinic? There should not be any dirt or stray medical supplies lying around. Don't be shy about asking to see all parts of the clinic. Your dog will no doubt have to be x-rayed at some point in his life, so asking to see the x-ray room is not an unreasonable request. Same goes for the operating room. If you're bringing home a puppy, he or she should be neutered or spayed in that room in the very near future.

Once you've made your clinic visits and evaluated all the information you've gathered, you need to make your final decision and book an appointment with the vet within 24 hours of your new dog coming home. It will take time to build a relationship with your vet, so don't be afraid to ask questions and get further clarifications on anything you don't fully understand. A good vet will always explain things in layman's terms to make sure you completely understand everything that's going on with your dog.

If possible, always book non-emergency appointments with the same veterinarian, as she will be the most familiar with your dog. This will also help build your relationship.

CHAPTER THREE

Know Your Responsibilities

Owning a dog comes with a lot of responsibilities. You have to feed him, ensure that he remains in good health, and provide him with opportunities for exercise and mental stimulation. Any dog left to his own devices can become a destructive dog.

Your house, including the back-yard, has to be suitable for your dog. If you have a large mixed breed, you must have a solid, high fence surrounding your yard. The gate must also have a secure lock. If you have a small dog, you have to make sure there's no space between the

Dog owners must always be informed about the local laws and requirements related to pet ownership. Check your local municipality's Web site for ordinances and other information that will help keep you and your dog in compliance with the law.

ground and the fence for him to crawl under, and there cannot be any holes in the fence.

Not only does your dog need to have good manners when he's in the house, he also has to mind his manners while he's in the backyard and when he's out walking around the neighborhood. If your dog is a chronic barker, you must bring him into the house after a reasonable amount of time outside so you don't anger your neighbors.

When you're walking with your dog, he must be on a leash unless you're in a designated leash-free zone. When you're in a leash-free park, make sure you know and follow the rules, which include picking up after him. You must also scoop his poop when he does his business while on your walk.

IDENTIFICATION

Every year, thousands of dogs are either stolen or lost, so your dog must have some form of identification. A collar with your dog's name and a phone number is a good idea, but refrain from putting your address

Dogs of all sizes must wear a collar with an identification tag. It's also a good idea for your dog to wear a tag indicating that he's received his mandated rabies shots.

FAST FACT

Pet theft is a real issue. In the United States, about one in five dogs will become lost or stolen. Dogs are stolen for any number of reasons, including for research purposes, for their fur, for dog fighting, and as food.

on the tag, as an unscrupulous person may be able to befriend your dog to get your address. You may want to put something like "requires medication" on the tag along with a phone number, so the person who finds your dog contacts you immediately.

While tags are the most common form of pet identification, they are not without problems. Collars and tags have a bad habit of falling off, and they can also be easily removed if someone steals your dog. There are several more permanent means of identification available which you might want to consider.

TATTOOS: One type of permanent identification is a tattoo. Dogs can be tattooed either inside an ear or on the inside of a thigh with a unique number that is then registered with a pet recovery organization like the National Dog Registry. While tattooing can be done at any time during a dog's life, it's usually done in the early weeks of a puppy's life. The problem with tattooing a dog is that if it's done when he's very young, the tattoo may become unreadable as he grows older.

MICROCHIPS: Another form of permanent identification is a microchip, which is a tiny computer chip implanted beneath your dog's skin, typically between his shoulder blades, by a veterinarian trained in the process. The microchip is non-toxic and has a unique number attached to it. If your mixed breed becomes lost and is brought to a veterinary clinic or shelter, the staff can scan the dog's back with a special microchip scanner to find his owner. Your information will come up, and the staff will contact you with your dog's whereabouts.

LICENSING

Most communities have laws requiring the licensing of dogs, and it's your duty as a responsible dog owner to comply with these laws. Licensing is a way for officials to keep track of the dogs that live in a community, make sure the dogs have been vaccinated against rabies, and return stray dogs to their owners. Not only do these laws make your community safer, they also help to protect your dog.

Nearly all municipalities have an animal control officer, who is responsible for issuing pet licenses and rounding up strays.

The cost of licensing your dog will depend on where you live. Check with your town, village, or city hall to find out what the licensing requirements are for your area. Most communities will impose a fine if your dog isn't licensed, so be sure to acquire a license as soon as you get your dog. At the same time, many cities offer discounted licensing fees to dogs that have been spayed or neutered.

SPAYING OR NEUTERING

If you've adopted your mixed-breed dog from a shelter or rescue organization, you're probably already aware of the ramifications of leaving a dog intact. Spaying females or neutering male dogs helps cut down on the enormous number of animals that end up unwanted and languishing in shelters.

In addition to population control, spaying and neutering each have some positive health benefits for dogs and their owners. An intact female can be bothersome to live with, as her hormones are constantly in flux. Females have about two heat cycles a year (every six to nine months, on average), during which she will discharge blood for about a month. This is a messy situation that can be easily avoided by spaying. Neutering a male dog will reduce his drive to roam. An intact male will do whatever he can—including digging under your fence or crossing busy streets—to get to a female in heat. A neutered male, on the other hand, is less likely to roam and will also be less inclined to hump anything and everything. He'll also be less likely to mark his territory with urine. In addition, neutering will curtail his aggressive behavior toward other dogs, which is important in a multi-dog house or if you plan to put your dog in doggy day care.

DISPELLING MYTHS

The best thing you can do as an individual to help combat the problem of pet overpopulation is to help dispel the following myths about spaying and neutering of pets:

Myth: Neutering or spaying will affect my dog's personality.

Truth: Your mixed breed will have the same personality after neutering or spaying. Sterilization surgery has no effect on personality, but it does help eliminate annoying sexual behaviors, such as roaming and marking territory (urinating) in the house.

Myth: Neutering or spaying will cause my dog to gain weight.

Truth: Weight gain in a healthy dog is strictly related to diet and exercise. Some dogs may become slightly less active after sterilization surgery, as they will not be expending as much energy on sexual matters, but a proper diet and adequate exercise will compensate for this.

Myth: It's better for my female dog to have one litter before spaying.

Truth: Having a litter prior to spaying has no health or behavioral benefits for your dog. On the contrary, there are serious health risks involved in pregnancy and birth, especially when things don't go exactly as nature intended.

Myth: Neutering my male dog will strip him of his masculinity.

Truth: Neutered male dogs still have typical male characteristics—larger size, broader head, and bolder personalities than females. The only male characteristics reduced or eliminated by neutering are undesirable ones: his desire to search for mates, his aggressive reaction to other male dogs, and his tendency to mark certain areas as his own.

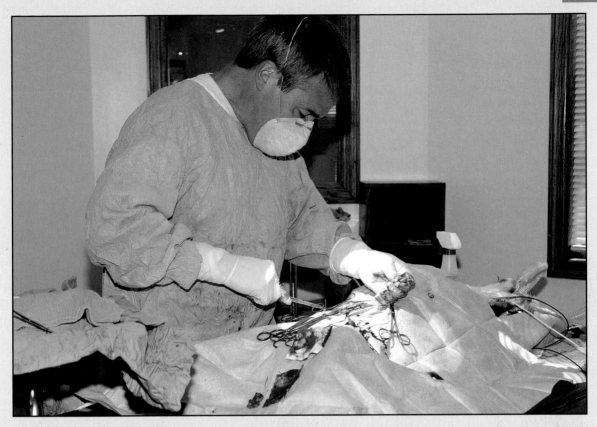

It's a wise idea to spay or neuter your mixed-breed dog. According to the Humane Society of the United States, one female dog and her offspring can theoretically produce up to 67,000 dogs in six years!

There are disease-prevention benefits to spaying and neutering as well. Spaying reduces your female mixed breed's chances of suffering from potentially fatal conditions such as ovarian cancer, uterine cancer, and pyometra, a life-threatening uterine infection. It also reduces her chances of suffering from mammary tumors. Neutering helps male dogs lower their risk of developing testicular cancer and most prostatic diseases.

Some people refuse to spay or neuter their dog because they have heard stories about deleterious side effects of the procedure, including personality changes or a tendency to become fat and lazy. There is a grain of truth in each of these stories, but for the most part such changes are negligible. Male dogs generally have a positive personality change, becoming less aggressive and having a diminished drive to roam looking for mates. The weight gain often

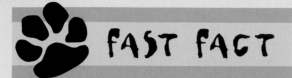

FAST FACT

You need to make provisions for your dog in your will. Consider who your mixed breed should live with, but make sure to ask that person before you designate her as your dog's guardian. You should also leave money in your will for the dog's guardian, to cover things like your dog's food and veterinary care.

cial constraints when it comes to spaying or neutering. Some local shelters also offer discounted prices for spaying and neutering, whether you adopted your dog from that shelter or somewhere else.

Dogs should be spayed or neutered between the ages of five and six months. If possible, a female should be spayed before her first heat cycle, usually around six months of age.

PET INSURANCE

Pet insurance has been available for over 20 years, but only in the past few years has it caught on among dog owners. Pet insurance provides peace of mind—for a small monthly payment, you know that if anything serious happens to your dog, such as an accident or a life-threatening

attributed to spaying or neutering may simply be a case of correlation, not causation. The procedure is most often done on young, active animals that are being fed a high-calorie diet. As a dog reaches adulthood, his metabolism slows and his dietary needs change. The weight gain some people see in their spayed or neutered dogs may just be the result of the slowed metabolism and improper diet, rather than having anything to do with the neutering. The best thing to do if you notice your dog gaining weight is to make sure he's receiving proper food and exercise.

Some people don't spay or neuter their dog because they believe they can't afford the procedure. Mindful of this concern, many veterinary clinics will make payment arrangements for people with finan-

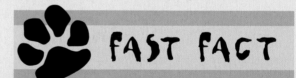

FAST FACT

According to a 2004 survey by the American Animal Hospital Association, only about 3 percent of Americans insure their pets. The percentage is much higher in some other countries, such as Sweden, where, according to market research publisher Packaged Facts, nearly 50 percent of pet owners insure their animals.

illness like cancer, the cost of his veterinary treatment will be covered. Pet insurance means that you don't have to make the difficult decision to treat your dog or put him down because the treatment is simply beyond your means. Some animals with chronic health conditions can require medications and constant care that rival the cost of health care for humans.

Depending on the genetic make-up of your mixed breed and how vigorous your activities with him are, you may decide to insure him as soon as you adopt him. People who have a less active lifestyle with their dogs may opt to forgo pet insurance altogether or wait until their mixed breed is older, when health problems generally start to occur. Like car and homeowner's insurance, your coverage, deductible, and rates will vary by company, so before you decide this is something you want to invest in, do some homework.

Situations typically covered by pet insurance policies include injuries and catastrophic illness coverage. Check with several insurance providers, as some policies may cover legal expenses related to your dog, as well as emergency boarding fees and vacation cancellation.

For the most part, elective procedures, such as teeth cleaning or

When walking in a public area, always pick up after your dog. Depending on where you live, the fines can be pretty hefty for leaving his droppings behind. More importantly, it shows consideration to others.

spaying or neutering, are not covered by insurance policies. Also not normally covered are annual vet visits and vaccinations. Preexisting medical conditions are also often excluded.

THE LAW AND YOUR MIXED BREED

We never want to get tangled up in the legal system because our dog bit another dog or a person. However, no matter how well trained we think our dogs may be, they are capable of snapping at any time. If you have an older dog, he may have some aggression triggers that no one was aware of before you adopted him. If this happens to you, bring your dog directly to a trainer or canine behaviorist to immediately work on modifying that behavior.

BARKING: You need to check what your city or state law is regarding excessive barking. For the most part, no specific laws prohibit excessive barking, so this will fall under the general nuisance or noise ordinance. For example, the local ordinance may prohibit loud or excessive noise after 11 P.M. If neighbors contin- ually complain to the police about a barking dog and the owner fails to do anything about it, she may be fined for disturbing the peace.

Some breeds, such as Shetland Sheepdogs and Pomeranians, are naturally more vocal than others. Whether or not your dog has one of these breeds in him, dogs bark for numerous reasons, including out of boredom, alarm, fear, or attention seeking. The most annoying bark— especially for neighbors who have to listen to it all day long while you're at work—is one that springs from boredom. Also detrimental to your relationship with your neighbors is the alarmist bark or the one that lets you know some- one's at the door.

Keeping your dog from barking excessively—particularly if you live in an apartment, a town- house, or another place where it might annoy your neigh- bors—is not only considerate, it is required by law in many communities.

PREVENTING AN ATTACK

The best ways to prevent your dog from being accused of biting a person or another dog are:

- train and socialize him
- never let him off leash unless in a designated off-leash area
- watch your mixed breed when he is around children

If a stranger approaches when you are on a walk, move out of his way, especially if your dog starts to get his hackles up. Post warning signs on your property, even if you own a small dog. Also, keep your dog's vaccinations up-to-date. You can never take too many precautions.

BITES: The most common reason that dog owners become entangled in the legal system is that their dog has bitten another dog or a person. According to the Centers for Disease Control in Atlanta, about 4.7 million people are bitten by a dog every year in the United States. Of those 4.7 million bite victims, 800,000 require some form of medical attention.

As your dog's owner, you are responsible for his actions, as well as for paying for any resulting medical costs. Depending on the severity of the bite and the litigiousness of the person who was bitten, the costs can be enormous. Don't be fooled into thinking this is only an issue for big dogs. Many little dogs can be just as aggressive, if not more so, and they can bite people with enough force to cause injury.

The best way to avoid this situation is to make sure that your dog never has the opportunity to cause harm to anyone. This is accomplished through proper training, as well as by making sure your dog is under control at all times, including when you're away from home or when he's in the care of other people.

CHAPTER FOUR

Bringing Your Mutt Home

Before your new family member comes home, you have to prepare your house, yourself, and your family for the lifestyle change that's about to take place. Once you know the day you will be bringing home your dog, plan to take some time off work. The more time you have to spend with your new dog when you first bring him home, the easier the transition will be for all of you. You'll also get him off to a great start in terms of housetraining.

Being home for the first week is ideal, but not always possible. So if you can take a few days off and make a long weekend out of the event, you're still going to give your

Before you bring a dog into your home, the entire family must be involved in preparing the living area and establishing the rules that the newcomer will be expected to follow.

dog a fine start. Be careful about bringing a dog home over the Christmas holiday. While you might be home during this time, there's generally so much going on that you won't have the opportunity to create a routine for your dog. And establishing a routine is imperative for training.

DOG-PROOFING YOUR HOME

Dogs are naturally curious and explore the world around them with their mouths. This means that, when given the opportunity, dogs will sniff, carry around, and chew a lot of things they shouldn't. It can cost a lot of money to replace damaged

shoes and furniture. Emergency trips to the veterinary clinic are not cheap, either.

The first thing you need to do is get down on your hands and knees and look at your home from dog's-eye level to see what kind of trouble your new arrival could cause. Then you need to remove any items of value or things that may be dangerous to your dog. Dangling cords from lamps, computers, televisions, and other appliances need to be tied up and hidden so your curious canine can't chew through them. If you can't stash the cords out of your dog's reach, spray a chew deterrent onto the cords. These products are

Cleaning supplies like these can be very dangerous to a curious puppy. Make sure they are locked in a cabinet, or kept in a spot that he can't reach.

all natural and taste terrible to most dogs, so they won't want to chew anything sprayed with them. These products can also be used on virtually everything, including chair and table legs, baseboards, and even your hands, which helps during your puppy's nipping phase.

You'll also need to clean off your floors. This means you can't leave magazines and newspapers lying around the living room and expect them to be readable when you come back 30 seconds later. Dogs love to shred paper, and they do it with amazing speed. If you have children, don't leave their toys lying around, either, especially if the toys have small pieces that can be easily swallowed by a dog and potentially cause him to choke. You also don't want your dog to turn all your children's

DANGEROUS PLANTS

Plants that are toxic to your mixed-breed dog can be found both indoors and outdoors. Some of the common plants to keep out of your dog's reach are listed in the table below:

Plant	Toxic Parts
Azaleas	Entire plant
Daffodil	Bulbs
Elephant's ear	Entire plant
English ivy	Entire plant
Foxglove	Leaves
Holly	Berries
Hyacinth	Bulbs
Iris	Leaves, roots
Lily of the valley	Leaves, flowers
Mistletoe	Berries
Philodendron	Entire plant
Poinsettia	Leaves, stem, flowers
Rhubarb	Leaves

For a full list of common poisonous plants, visit the Humane Society of the United States Web site, www.hsus.org.

toys into his own. A good rule of thumb to follow is this: if it's on the floor, it belongs to the dog. So put your children's toys in a room and close the door so the dog can't get to them.

If your home is filled with lots of fresh-cut flowers and plants, you need to do some research to determine if they're toxic to dogs. Dogs love to nibble on greenery, so wherever possible, place any plants out of reach. Some potentially toxic houseplants include the asparagus fern, the Boston ivy, the calla lily, and the philodendron.

OFF-LIMITS AREAS

Before your puppy or adult dog comes home, you need to determine which rooms he'll be allowed into and which ones will be strictly off-limits. Most likely, he'll have free rein in your bedroom, where he may sleep at night in the crate, as well as in the kitchen and the living room. No dog should be allowed to roam the whole house at will until he's fully housetrained.

In your bedroom, pick up your clothes, put your dirty laundry in the closet, and shut the closet door. Your shoes also need to go in the closet. Dogs love to chew items that smell like their owners, especially dirty laundry and expensive shoes. So be

sure to clean under your bed, especially if you're bringing home a puppy or a small mixed breed, as he'll be small enough to get under there and get into trouble.

Kitchens and bathrooms are filled with toxic products. Even though these are usually kept in the cupboards, dogs can be crafty when given the opportunity and can pry open a cupboard door and get into the cleaners. Keep the cupboard doors securely closed with child locks. In the bathroom, keep the toilet lid down so your dog doesn't develop a habit of drinking from the toilet bowl. You may initially need to

Garages should be off-limits to your dog, as they often contain dangerous tools as well as toxic products like antifreeze and paint thinner.

put the toilet paper out of your dog's reach as well: a dangling piece of toilet paper makes for a great toy. Dogs love to grab the dangling piece and run around the house with it. Also make sure that your garbage cans are kept in securely closed cupboards; dogs love to scour through the garbage for scraps. These rules apply to all dogs, no matter what their size. A small dog is just as capable of pawing open a cupboard door or knocking over a garbage can as a larger dog.

Harmful products are not only found in kitchens and bathrooms. Garages and basements house all kinds of toxic hazards, such as old paint cans, mouse traps and insecticides, antifreeze, paint, fertilizer, motor oil, and turpentine, all of which can be potentially dangerous, if not fatal, to a dog. Restricting your dog's access to the basement and the garage throughout his life is the safest strategy.

BACKYARD

No doubt your new dog will be spending a lot of time playing outside in the backyard. A dog should not be left outside for hours on end, but it's okay to let him play and nap unsupervised for short periods, as long as the yard is fenced and dog-proofed.

Your yard must have a fence high enough to prevent your dog from jumping over it. The fence must also be sturdy enough that he can't push his way through loose boards or tunnel under it and escape.

To puppy-proof your backyard, you first need to remove all poisonous plants as well as dangerous and toxic lawn and garden products. Is your fence secure from top to bottom? Dogs can be jumpers, so your fence needs to be at least six feet (1.8 meters) high. Make sure there are no chairs or tables placed near the fence that the dog could use as a launching pad.

The bottom of your fence also needs to be flush with the ground. If there are any spaces between the fence and the ground, your puppy or small dog will do his best to wiggle through them and explore the neighbor's backyard. Perform regular maintenance on the fence so your dog can't escape through loose boards or holes. You also need to affix a lock to the gate to deter strangers from coming into the yard and making off with your dog.

If you have a pool or hot tub in your backyard, you must enclose it with a strong wooden or chain-link fence and never let your dog into the backyard without proper supervision. Pool covers are particularly dangerous because they trick the dog into thinking the surface is solid. He may walk out onto the cover and sink. The cover can then collapse around the dog and suffocate him.

You need to decide if your dog is going to have a designated bathroom area in a relatively secluded corner of the yard, or if he's going to be able to freely eliminate on your nice green lawn.

SUPPLIES YOU'LL NEED

Not only do you have to clean up your house and yard in preparation for your new addition to the family, you also have to buy some very important supplies, such as toys, food, bowls, treats, beds, and a crate, especially if he's a puppy. If you're bringing home a puppy, you'll also need a lot of paper towels and a good enzymatic cleaner, since there will be a lot of accidents to clean up. Avoid using a cleaner that contains ammonia, which is a component of urine; its scent will continually attract your puppy to that same off-limits spot.

When used properly, crates make a wonderful housetraining tool as well as a safe place for your puppy or dog to go to when you can't supervise him. It's akin to a playpen for children. Both plastic and metal crates are available for indoor use.

Hard plastic crates come in various sizes, so if you're bringing home a puppy that will grow into a larger dog, you'll have to buy one or two to get you through the entire housetraining phase. Buying a plastic crate

Your puppy will quickly take to the idea of the crate as his "den," and will not mind spending time there. However, be sure not to pen him up in the crate for too long.

for your puppy that will also comfortably house your large adult dog is not wise. Initially, it will be too big and will hamper the potty training that it's supposed to facilitate. However, if you have a puppy that won't grow too large, you may be able to use one crate. Some plastic or wire crates come with a barrier that can be moved to change the dimensions inside, accommodating your dog as he grows.

Dogs have a natural instinct not to eliminate where they sleep and eat. Therefore, when it's the correct size, a crate teaches a puppy to hold his bladder for as long as he possibly can and become accustomed to regular bathroom breaks. If the crate is too large, your puppy can go to the bathroom in a corner and then just avoid that area.

Plastic crates, while serviceable, don't allow your dog to easily see what's going on around him, which may make him feel isolated from the family. Wire crates, on the other hand, allow your dog to see all around him, so he feels like he's part of the action without being in the middle of it. No matter how large your dog is, the crate must enable him to easily stand up, turn around, and stretch out.

THE BIG DAY

When you're driving to pick up a dog from a breeder or a shelter, make sure to bring a crate for him to ride in on the way home. If you can, get an old towel or some other piece of fabric from his last home that has a familiar scent on it and place it in the crate. This will help make the separation a little less stressful. You should also have a leash and collar when you pick up your new dog. He will have to relieve himself immediately, so you'll need to let him out of his crate.

When you first bring your dog or puppy home, keep him on a leash when he's not in areas you have fully dog-proofed or puppy-proofed. It will take months before you can allow him to freely roam around the house, because he first needs to be taught the rules.

WHAT TO EXPECT THE FIRST FEW NIGHTS

The first few days and nights following your new dog's arrival will be overwhelming, tiring, confusing, frustrating, but, above all, wonderful. By doing your research, dog-proofing your home, and having the necessary supplies on hand for his arrival, you have done all you can to prepare yourself for the playful bundle of fur that's coming into your life. Depending on your mixed breed's background, he may have no training at all and may not even know his name. There are many things you'll have to slowly and patiently teach him. As time goes by, you'll notice that he responds to his name when you call him, sits when you ask him to, and eliminates in his designated outside location. Be patient, however: this won't happen overnight.

While the first night may be the worst for everyone, since your dog is confused and overwhelmed, there are a few things you can do to make things a little less stressful. Put your dog's crate beside your bed, so he knows that someone even a little bit familiar is close. This will comfort him to some extent. If you're bringing home a puppy, place a warm water bottle wrapped in a towel in the crate with him to simulate the warmth of curling up with littermates. The shelter may give you a piece of cloth or blanket that retains the scent of your puppy's mother. There are also dog toys with a warmer and heartbeat available that may help your puppy feel less lonely.

THE INITIAL HEALTH SCREENING

Within the first 24 to 48 hours of bringing your dog home, you need to take him to the vet for an exam. This first visit introduces your new dog to

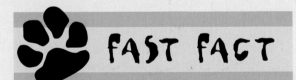

FAST FACT

You can help your little guy adjust to his new home by enforcing your household rules from the very beginning. Although it will take a lot of repetition before your puppy learns everything he needs to know, consistency from the start will help him develop a sense of security and a close bond with you. Try to devote a lot of time to your puppy during these first critical days.

your veterinary clinic in a friendly and nonthreatening manner. It will give your dog a positive first impression of the vet, the clinic, and its staff. You'll also be asked to fill out forms detailing your contact information and your dog's gender, color, age, and so on. Be sure to arrive for your appointment a few minutes early so you have enough time to complete the paperwork.

When you go for this visit, bring whatever paperwork on the dog you may have, no matter how limited the information is. You should also bring a stool sample. The sample will enable the vet to check your dog for parasites.

The veterinarian will perform an extensive exam to ensure that your dog is healthy. She will check your mixed breed's heart, lungs, eyes, and the range of motion in his limbs. If you have a puppy, your vet will go through his vaccination schedule with you; over the next four months, your puppy will receive numerous inoculations to help him fend off diseases like parvovirus, distemper, and rabies.

CHAPTER FIVE

Health Issues Your Mutt May Face

Some people believe that mixed-breed dogs are far healthier than purebreds. After all, they say, mutts don't have to worry about the genetic disorders that plague so many purebreds as a result of inbreeding. Is this fact or fiction?

It's actually a little bit of both. When people tout the superior health of a mixed breed, they are no doubt basing their belief on the hybrid vigor theory that essentially states

Understanding the health problems that may afflict your mixed-breed dog, and learning how to prevent or mitigate them, is essential to keeping your canine pal happy and healthy.

that a creature from mixed DNA will inherit the best traits of its parents. This theory holds that the wider the gene pool, the lower the likelihood of genetic predispositions to illness.

It's impossible to determine if mixed-breed dogs have fewer health problems than purebreds because no one keeps health statistics for mixed breeds. What can be conclusively stated, however, is that every dog breed can develop genetic diseases. Keep in mind, too, that no individual dog, mixed or pure, is immune to the effects of distemper, injuries, parasites, and rabies.

There are no specific diseases one mixed breed is more prone to than others. If you know something about your mixed breed's parentage, however, this may give you important clues. For example, if your dog has some Labrador Retriever in him, then he may be genetically predisposed to suffer from conditions like hip dysplasia. Dogs that are part Terrier may be prone to any number of hereditary eye disorders, including entropion, a defect that causes the eyelids to roll inward and cause irritation. Because of the wide range of illnesses that can occur in mixed breeds, it makes more sense for a new owner to focus her attention on illnesses and conditions that any dog can contract.

Mixed breeds with a parent or two from an active larger breed, like Boxer, Lab, or German Shepherd mixes, may be genetically prone to physical problems like hip dysplasia.

ALLERGIES

More and more dogs are suffering from allergies; whether these are caused by the environment or genetics is not known. What we do know is that they are very uncomfortable for the dog.

FOOD ALLERGIES: Many dogs are now allergic to certain ingredients in their food. Corn, wheat, beef, soy, and lamb are all common sources of food allergens. A dog suffering from a food allergy will often have skin irritations, like hot spots, or chronic stomach problems. To discover which specific ingredient is causing the reaction, your veterinarian will put your dog on a hypoallergenic diet that contains a protein source your dog has never eaten before, such as duck, fish, or venison. The food will also contain an unusual carbohydrate source, such as barley or potato. Your dog will be on this diet for several weeks, after which you will slowly introduce potentially problematic ingredients to determine if they are the allergen source or not.

ENVIRONMENTAL ALLERGIES: Dogs, like people, can suffer from environmental allergies. If the irritation is environmental in origin, the symptoms, which most commonly appear as skin irritations, will manifest themselves seasonally and then subside. If the allergic reaction is chemical-based, it will often show itself after an encounter with the offending ingredient. For example, your dog may become very itchy following a bath. If that's the case, chances are he's allergic to something in the shampoo you're using. Many dogs are also allergic to plastics and the dyes used in them. You may think the allergic reaction is food-based, but if he eats or drinks from a plastic bowl, the bowl may actually be the source of his allergy.

BLOAT WITH TORSION

One of the most serious medical conditions to which larger dogs are prone is called bloat. This condition is most common in dogs over 40 pounds (18 kg). When a dog suffers from bloat, his stomach becomes distended because of a buildup of gas and foamy mucus. The pressure of the gas causes the stomach to expand inside the abdominal cavity and press against the heart, lungs, and abdominal blood vessels. By impinging on these internal organs, the bloated stomach restricts their function and creates a painful and terrifying situation for the dog.

Bloat can quickly become a life-threatening emergency, particularly if

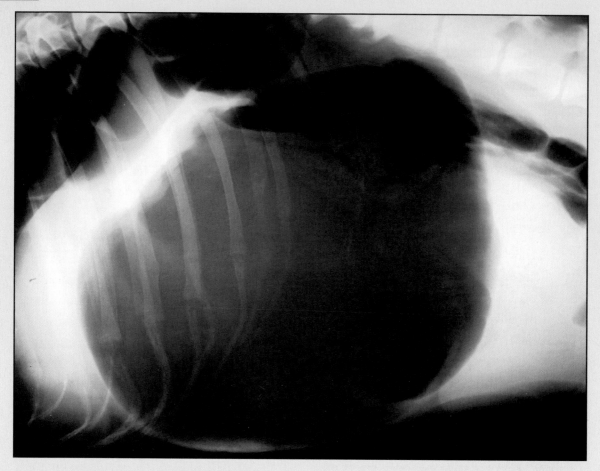

This x-ray shows what happens when a dog suffers from bloat. The large dark area in the center is gas trapped in a German Shepherd's stomach. Bloat with torsion will be fatal unless your dog receives immediate medical care.

it's accompanied by torsion. Torsion is a rotation of the stomach that pinches off its entrance from the esophagus and its exit through the duodenum. This traps water, food, gas, and foam, causing the stomach to swell even more. The blood builds up carbon dioxide because the inner abdominal pressure prevents the heart and lungs from doing their jobs of cleansing and oxygenating the blood. The dog's blood pressure drops, his body becomes toxic, and the stomach continues to become painfully distended. Bloat with torsion is almost always fatal, unless emergency medical attention is immediately sought.

Dogs with deep chests, such as the Great Dane, the Bull Mastiff, and most retriever breeds, are especially susceptible to bloat, but there are steps you can take to minimize the risk. Soak your dog's kibble in water before you feed it to him; this will allow the kibble to expand in the bowl, rather than in your dog's stomach. You could try placing large chew toys in the bowl with the kibble, to slow down your dog's eating. You also want your dog to rest for 30 minutes following a meal. Then take him outside. Once he has done his business, bring him back in the house and have him lay on his bed. This is a routine you should start from the first meal. He will quickly catch on and oblige.

VACCINATIONS

During his first few months of life, your puppy should be scheduled to receive injections to protect him against a number of infectious diseases. These include parvovirus, distemper, and rabies. Adult dogs need vaccine boosters to maintain their immunity. Your vet will set up a schedule of vaccinations for your dog. These vaccinations will protect your dog from a number of diseases, including canine parvovirus, distemper, infectious canine hepatitis, parainfluenza, and rabies.

VACCINATION SCHEDULE FOR PUPPIES

The following vaccination schedule is recommended by the American Animal Hospital Association:

Vaccine	Age of Puppy
Distemper	8 weeks and 12 weeks
Parvovirus	8 weeks, 12 weeks, 16 weeks
Parainfluenza	8 weeks, 12 weeks
Coronavirus	8 weeks, 12 weeks
Canine adenovirus-2	8 weeks, 12 weeks
Leptospirosis	8 weeks, 12 weeks
Bordetella*	12 weeks
Lyme disease*	12 weeks, 16 weeks
Rabies +	16 weeks

* Optional vaccines, depending on location and risk.   + Required by law.

Source: American Animal Hospital Association

CANINE PARVOVIRUS: Also known as parvo, this disease is highly infectious, and its effects can include severe vomiting, bloody diarrhea, a high fever, dehydration, and depression. The disease has a 50 percent mortality rate.

Parvo is transmitted through fecal matter and can live in the soil for up to a year. It can also survive on the bottom of your shoes and on dogs' paws for upwards of 10 days.

DISTEMPER: This is another potentially fatal disease. Distemper, which is highly contagious, is transmitted through the air and by contact. Symptoms of distemper are a yellowish-gray discharge from your dog's nose and eyes, accompanied by a dry cough, lethargy, and a fever. Other symptoms include vomiting, diarrhea, and a loss of appetite. As the disease progresses, it can attack the dog's intestinal tract and nervous system, resulting in seizures and convulsions.

INFECTIOUS CANINE HEPATITIS: Formally called canine adenovirus-1, infectious canine hepatitis is a virus that targets a dog's liver and kidneys. It is often spread through the air, but can also be ingested by the dog. Symptoms can range from mild fever and lethargy to jaundice, shock, and death. The potential seriousness of this disease is enough to put it on the list of "must-haves" among canine vaccinations.

PARAINFLUENZA: Canine parainfluenza is a respiratory illness similar to the human cold virus. It is spread through the air and through secretions, and it causes coughing, a nasal discharge, and bronchial inflammation. Even though it is not generally considered serious, parainfluenza can make your dog miserable and can lead to other conditions such as kennel cough or pneumonia.

RABIES: All municipalities in North America require dogs to be vaccinated against rabies, because it's almost always fatal to both dogs and

Federal and state laws require dogs to be vaccinated against rabies.

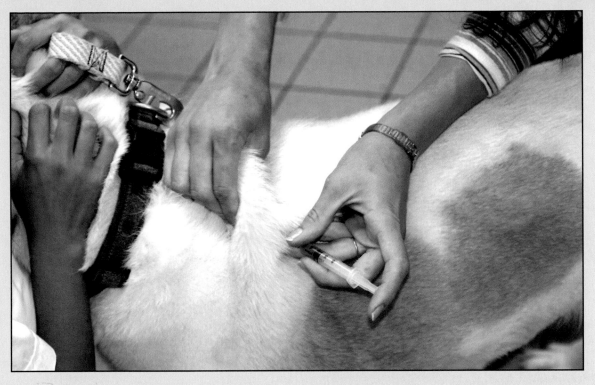

Not all veterinarians follow the same vaccination schedule, and some municipalities require shots that other communities don't. The safest thing is to follow your vet's advice with regard to your dog's vaccinations.

humans. A person can contract rabies by coming into contact with a rabid dog's saliva, either through a bite or if the rabid dog's saliva enters a person's open wound in some other way. There are rabies vaccinations for humans, but they must be administered within 14 days of infection.

There are actually two forms of rabies, both of which attack a dog's central nervous system. The so-called dumb, or paralytic, form of rabies causes paralysis of the dog's throat, resulting in excessive drooling and the inability to swallow. This creates the "frothing at the mouth" associated with the disease. The other form, furious rabies, involves the infected dog going "mad" and becoming vicious. Furious rabies will cause paralysis and eventually death.

Rabies vaccines are available in a one-year and a three-year inoculation. Either vaccination can be given to a puppy as young as three months of age. Check the laws in your state and municipality regarding rabies vaccinations for your dog. Your veterinarian will have all that information.

CANINE TICK-BORNE DISEASES

Following are some diseases that can result from tick bites:

Lyme disease: Causes various degrees of joint swelling, arthritis, fevers, and fatigue.

Ehrlichiosis: Symptoms include anemia, high fever, and lethargy.

Tick paralysis: Characterized by a lack of coordination of the rear limbs, which may progress to complete paralysis of the rear legs.

Rocky Mountain spotted fever: Obviously causes a fever, but is also known to cause loss of appetite, vomiting, diarrhea, muscle and joint aches, anemia, and neurological symptoms, such as dizziness and seizures.

Babesiosis: Known to cause fever, anemia, weakness, depression, dehydration, and shock.

OTHER VACCINATIONS: If you plan to put your dog into doggy day care, you may be required to give him a bordetella vaccine, which will help him stave off kennel cough. Kennel cough is a highly infectious airborne disease. It will not harm a healthy adult dog, but it can be dangerous to a puppy. It is characterized by a dry, hacking cough. The bordetella vaccine is administered in two doses—one when the puppy is between six and eight weeks of age, and another one when he is between 10 and 12 weeks old.

Some veterinarians will vaccinate dogs for canine coronavirus. This is a gastrointestinal disease that upsets the digestive system; it is typically accompanied by vomiting and diarrhea. Coronavirus is spread by contact with an infected dog or its feces.

HEREDITARY MUSCULOSKELETAL AND NERVOUS SYSTEM DISEASES

The most common genetic problems seen in dogs today are hip dysplasia, elbow dysplasia, luxating patella, and epilepsy. Each of these affect both mixed-breed dogs and purebreds. Because mixed breeds are of unknown origin, though, it is often difficult to tell that there is a problem before the condition has fully developed.

HIP DYSPLASIA: Hip dysplasia is a hereditary disease that is typically caused by genetics and environmental factors. This debilitating disease, which is most commonly found in large dogs, is the number one cause of canine arthritis.

In a nutshell, hip dysplasia occurs when one of two things happens: (1) the dog's femur head is not being held in place correctly by a concave socket in the pelvis known as the acetabulum, or (2) either the acetabulum or the femur head, is misshapen instead of smooth and round, which causes abnormal wear and tear within the joint whenever the dog moves. There is no cure for hip dysplasia, but there are medications a vet can prescribe to alleviate the dog's pain.

ELBOW DYSPLASIA AND OSTEOCHONDRITIS DISSECANS:

Elbow dysplasia is a hereditary disease in which the elbow joints are malformed. Elbow dysplasia is traditionally treated with anti-inflammatory medication or surgery, depending on its severity.

Osteochondritis dissecans (OCD) occurs when the cartilage thickens around the joint area. This thickened cartilage is quite prone to damage and has the potential to tear and form a flap or reattach to the bone. A flap of cartilage may even form over the elbow, which can be very painful for the dog. OCD can occur in one or many joints and usually begins to manifest itself when the dog is between four and eight months of age. The chief sign of OCD is lameness following activity.

LUXATING PATELLA: A luxating patella, which is a painful condition, occurs when the dog's kneecap slips out of place. This can only be corrected by surgery.

EPILEPSY: Epilepsy, a brain disorder characterized by physical convulsions or seizures, is generally hereditary. As in humans, the trigger for an epileptic seizure in a dog may or may not be identifiable. But before concluding that the seizures are caused by an unknown stimulus, you and your veterinarian first have to rule out all other triggers, such as calcium imbalances, head trauma, internal obstructions, liver problems, overheating, parasites, poisoning, tick paralysis, and vitamin deficiencies. Depending on the severity of the seizures, your veterinarian may prescribe medication.

EYE DISEASES

Just like purebred dogs, mixed breeds are susceptible to congenital and hereditary eye diseases, which all have the potential to lead to blindness. These include cataracts, various problems with the eyelid, glaucoma, and progressive retinal atrophy (PRA).

CATARACTS: This is when the lens of the eye clouds over. The lens may only have a small cloudy dot on it or the entire lens may become opaque, causing complete blindness. Cataracts are typically associated with old age, but they can occur in younger dogs as well. This condition is hereditary.

ECTROPION: This occurs when the lower eyelid drops and exposes the interior of the lid. If the condition is relatively mild, it can be treated with veterinarian-prescribed antibiotics, a corticosteriod ointment, or eye drops. But if it's more severe, surgery may be necessary.

ENTROPION: This is when the dog's eyelid turns inward toward the eye, which causes the eyelashes or fur around the eye to rub against the eyeball. This is obviously irritating to the dog and can be surgically corrected.

GLAUCOMA: As in humans, glaucoma occurs when the body produces too much fluid inside the eyeball, which then builds up and creates pressure on the eye. Symptoms include extreme redness or a cloudy appearance to the eye. If glaucoma treatment fails, removal of the eye is generally the best option for the dog, because often by the time this condition is diagnosed the dog has probably already lost sight in that eye.

PROGRESSIVE RETINAL ATROPHY (PRA): PRA is a hereditary condition that involves the gradual loss of sight because the retina's light-sensitive cells, located at the back of the eye, are slowly deteriorating. Early signs of the disease include night blindness, but as the disease progresses the dog will also lose his ability to see in daylight.

One way to tell if your dog has this disease is to check his pupils. The pupils will constantly be dilated in an attempt to take in more light. You may also notice the lens of his eye becoming cloudy or opaque, as the disease causes the eye to look like the dog has cataracts. Blind dogs function very well in situations with which they're familiar, so don't move the furniture around if your dog is losing his eyesight.

HEART PROBLEMS

A dog can suffer from minor heart ailments, such as a murmur, to serious conditions that cause sudden death, all of which can be hereditary or congenital. Congenital heart disease is present at birth and can include heart malformations or malformations of the vessels surrounding the heart. As a dog gets older, his congenital heart condition will get worse.

Subaortic stenosis (SAS) has no outwardly visible symptoms, and dogs with this condition may die unexpectedly. SAS is caused by the narrowing of the left ventricle, which is just below the aortic valve. When stenosis occurs, the heart has to work harder in order to push blood through the ever-narrowing opening.

A heart murmur is a common symptom of SAS. However, murmurs can be difficult to detect without a Doppler echocardiogram or a cardiac catheterization. There is currently no treatment for this disease.

HYPOTHYROIDISM

This condition occurs when a dog's thyroid gland is not producing enough thyroid hormone. A dog suffering from this condition may be lethargic; have a dull, dry, or thinning coat; gain weight easily; and have areas of the body that are warmer than others.

Some forms of hypothyroidism are hereditary. In other cases, the problem develops as the dog ages. This condition can be detected through a blood test, and can be treated with medication.

❧❧❧❧

All dogs, no matter how mixed their gene pool, are susceptible to certain diseases. Because mixed-breed dogs often have such a muddied background, it's impossible to know exactly which diseases, if any, a particular dog may be at risk of developing. Don't let fear of potential medical problems prevent you from getting a mixed-breed dog, however, as many of these dogs will remain healthy throughout their lifetimes.

CHAPTER SIX

Caring for Your Puppy

Your puppy is going to go through a lot of physical, social, and intellectual changes during his first six months of life. Think of this as comparable to a child's infancy, terrible twos, adolescence, and puberty—all within a six-month time frame instead of 16 years.

When your mixed-breed puppy comes home, he'll be in the midst of his infancy stage (eight to 12 weeks of age). During this stage in his life, he's solely concerned with satisfying his basic needs: eating, sleeping, eliminating, and playing. Don't expect much during these first few weeks. If he comes to you when you call his name two days in a row, consider yourself lucky. For the most part, however, he won't be able to

During his first few months your puppy will have a lot to learn. Be patient with him.

remember anything from one day to the next.

Between eight and ten weeks of age, your puppy will go through the fear-impression period of his emotional development. All of a sudden, puppies can become afraid of anything and everything. If this reaction goes unchecked, your fearful puppy can grow up to become a very anxious dog, which is dangerous. Fearful dogs bite as a way to protect themselves.

To help minimize your puppy's fears, teach your children to treat the puppy carefully. Don't let them chase him or attack him with noisy items like the vacuum. Most important, when your puppy exhibits a fear of something, don't coddle, pet, or comfort him. He'll think you're also frightened of the object or situation, and that fear is the proper response. Ignore his fear and let your puppy investigate the situation on his own terms. It may take a few tries, but with patience, he'll overcome these fears.

THREE TO FOUR MONTHS OF AGE

Around 12 weeks of age, your easy-going, happy-go-lucky, follow-you-around-everywhere puppy will

Small children must be carefully supervised when handling puppies to make sure they do not accidentally injure the dogs.

become more comfortable with his surroundings. He'll become braver and bolder. During this phase, which is akin to a child's terrible twos, he'll become very demanding. He'll want to be the center of attention at all times and will do whatever it takes to grab the spotlight. This can include pawing at you while you're watching TV or going into the laundry hamper and bringing your underwear to you, even if you're entertaining dinner guests.

To a puppy, any attention is good, whether you're praising him or scolding him, so you're better off ignoring the bad and praising the good. At

this point in his maturation, he'll also test your position as the household's top dog. Your puppy instinctively wants to overthrow you and become the pack leader. He'll challenge you every chance he gets, but you can't let him win.

This is where puppy school comes in. At around three months old, believe it or not, your puppy's brain is fully developed and he's starting to learn things, both good and bad. Some will be the things you've taught him, but he's also learned many things on his own.

It's important to start training him to do what you want him to do. He'll act like a tough guy, but he's still young and impressionable enough to be taught right from wrong. With diligent training and strict enforcement of household rules, you'll be shaping your dog's behavior for the better.

Don't get complacent, however. Your puppy will soon decide that obedience is no longer on his to-do list. This personality flip usually occurs at around five months of age.

It is up to you to make sure that as your curious puppy explores the world around him, his experiences are safe and positive. Scary encounters with people or other dogs in the first few months may cause your puppy pal to become overly fearful.

This is the equivalent of a child's adolescent phase. Just as teenagers can be bratty, defiant, and strong-willed, so too can a five-month-old or six-month-old dog.

How do you know you've hit the "teenage period?" Instead of walking amicably beside you as you go around the block, your dog will now pull you around the neighborhood. He also won't come when he's called. Instead, he'll look at you when you call him, then take off in the opposite direction. When you correct him, his bad behavior might actually become worse.

It's important for you to continue to attend obedience classes during this phase or, at the very least, maintain a regular training schedule at home. Even though he may not seem like he's listening, the lessons will help to remind your dog who's really the boss. You may not think you can get through this phase, but you will. Be patient. He'll eventually come back around.

PUPPY NUTRITION

When puppies are born, they nurse from their mother every two hours, but by the time they're seven weeks old they should be eating only dry puppy kibble. When you go to pick up your puppy from the caregiver, she may supply you with a bit of the food she has been feeding the puppies for the past few weeks. If she doesn't give you any of the kibble he's been eating, find out what kind it is and make sure to have some on hand before his next meal. It's important to keep your new puppy on the same diet for the first few days to avoid an upset stomach. You may also want to get a container of

PROPER PET TREATS

Bones are great to give to dogs who love to chew. However, never give a dog chicken or turkey bones. They are so soft that a dog can break them easily, and bone splinters can cause serious injury to the dog's throat and digestive tract.

Any time you decide to give a dog a bone or a rawhide chew, he should be supervised. Some dogs may not chew these items properly; others may be able to break them apart. Either way, the dog could choke.

the caregiver's water to mix in with yours for the same reason.

Over time, you may decide to change your puppy's food. There is no one brand that is best for a particular type of dog, so you'll have to do some research. Talk to your local pet supply store staff and ask what they recommend for your mixed breed. Their recommendations will be based on product quality and customer feedback, as well as on the size and makeup of your dog.

When you read the dog food label, look for an American Association of Feed Control Officials (AAFCO) stamp of approval. This means the food is nutritionally balanced and complete, according to the AAFCO guidelines. AAFCO

Although you should only set food out for your puppy at mealtimes, he must have access to fresh water throughout the day.

foods must contain certain vitamins and minerals in proper proportion. If the label doesn't state that the food meets the AAFCO guidelines, then keep looking.

You should also choose a food that is specifically formulated for larger or smaller breeds of puppies, depending on what you think you have. A large-breed puppy is defined as a breed of dog that will grow to weigh more than 50 pounds (23 kg) as an adult. Small or medium dogs are less than 50 pounds, while an adult toy dog is defined as weighing less than five pounds (2.2 kg). Food for large-breed puppies contains less calcium compared to foods for puppies of smaller breeds, which helps large-breed puppies grow at a slow and steady rate. This will lessen their chances of suffering from musculoskeletal disorders. Growing too quickly will increase the likelihood that your large-breed puppy will one day suffer from one of these debilitating conditions.

Make sure the food you choose is made from high-quality ingredients. At least two types of meat should be listed among the first five ingredients—dogs are carnivores and require a meat-based diet. You may notice that vegetable-based kibble—which is made mostly of rice, wheat, and corn—is less expensive per bag

A DOG'S SENSES

Dogs have fewer than 2,000 taste buds, compared to humans' 9,000. It's the smell, not the taste, that attracts a dog to food. A dog's sense of smell is so good because he has 200 million scent receptors as compared to our 5 million. So don't worry that feeding your dog the same food day in and day out for years may bore your dog. He can't really taste it anyway.

than meat-based food. However, vegetable-based foods are more expensive in the long run, because you will have to feed your dog more of the lesser-quality food per meal in order to meet his nutritional requirements. Vegetable diets are also very high in carbohydrates, which are difficult for dogs to digest.

You should also check how the food is preserved. Today, most dog foods are naturally preserved with vitamin E and, in some cases, with vitamin C. Avoid foods that use chemical preservatives, such as ethoxyquin, as these can actually be harmful to dogs.

TYPES OF PUPPY FOOD

There are a number of dog-food options for your mutt. These include dry kibble, frozen food, semisoft food, and canned food. Most dogs are fed a dry kibble–based diet, because this is convenient and

economical. Kibble also has the added benefit of helping to clean your dog's teeth. As your dog chews, the hard kibble scrapes plaque and tartar off his tooth enamel.

If you want to feed your dog natural foods, you may want to consider feeding him a frozen diet. These foods are made with fresh meat, vegetables, and fruit, and contain nothing artificial. The food is easy to dole out, since it can be cut into chunks. Be aware, however, that frozen dog food is expensive, and it's not always easy to find.

Other options are canned and semisoft foods. Canned foods can be nutritionally complete, because they're made with one or two types of muscle meats or poultry, as well as animal by-products, grains, vitamins, and minerals. Canned food is great when combined with a puppy's kibble if he's having difficulties chewing; this may be the case when he is losing his teeth, which usually occurs when a puppy is between four and six months old. However, canned and semisoft foods are high in calories and fat, and they are also expensive.

Semisoft foods are not as solid as kibble but not as soft as canned dog food. However, semisoft food is a serious downgrade from other types of dog food because it's made with sugar, animal tissues, grains, and fats, rather than high-quality proteins and fats. Avoid giving your puppy this type of food as his main nutritional source, because it's essentially junk food. Feeding your dog a poor-quality diet can lead to nutritional deficiencies, which can manifest themselves through dry skin, poor coat, and potential behavioral issues.

Semisoft and canned foods also don't help reduce a dog's plaque and tartar buildup, so if you feed your dog a soft diet, you may find yourself having to pay your vet for a professional tooth cleaning on a regular basis.

Another extremely important thing to consider is whether or not your dog likes the food. Most dogs will eat virtually anything, so if yours turns up his nose at the food, try another kind. If he does this with multiple brands of food, however, head to the vet; his lack of appetite could signal a health problem.

For most puppies, dry kibble is the best option. It's economical, and provides the added benefit of helping to clean your dog's teeth. As he chews, the hard kibble will scrape plaque and tartar off the tooth enamel.

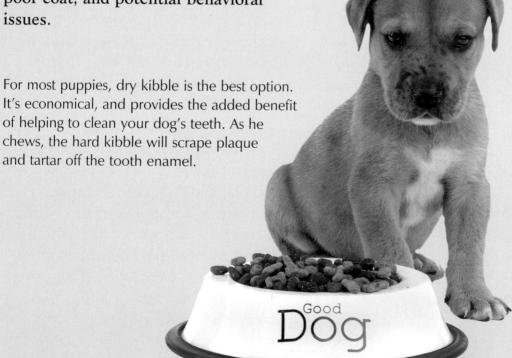

CANINE FIRST AID

When a dog joins your family, it's important to have canine first aid supplies on hand. Your canine first aid kit should contain the following items:

- gauze pads
- antibiotic ointment
- hydrogen peroxide
- petroleum jelly
- eye wash
- ear wash
- medications
- sterile stretch gauze
- bandage scissors

- splints
- a blanket
- tweezers
- tensor bandage
- copies of the dog's health records (such as CERF or OFA certification and other paperwork)

- bismuth tablets
- rectal thermometer
- medications
- local and national poison control numbers
- phone numbers for your regular veterinary clinic and the emergency clinic.

FEEDING

Puppies must be fed at regular intervals. Initially, your mixed-breed puppy will need to be fed three times a day at breakfast, lunch, and dinner. Between five and six months of age, you can start feeding your puppy twice a day: breakfast and dinner. Make the transition gradually over a one-week period by slowly decreasing the amount of food you give him at lunch and increasing his food allotment in the morning and evening.

Never put a bowl of food down in the morning and allow your puppy to pick at it throughout the day. This is called free feeding. Your dog probably won't graze; instead, regardless of his size, your puppy should wolf down everything that's put in front of him in a matter of minutes. Free feeding isn't advisable for another reason as well. You need to always remind your dog that you're the boss, and a surefire way to do this is by being his food source. This will be of particular importance when your dog is going through his terrible twos and adolescent phases—two times during his first six months that he'll challenge your authority.

SOCIALIZATION

In order for your puppy to grow up and become a well-adjusted adult dog, you must expose him to every kind of person, household noise, and social situation that you can imagine. If you don't properly socialize your puppy, you run the risk that your puppy will grow into a fearful or aggressive adult dog. This can be

It is important for your puppy to get out and meet other people and animals.

dangerous when you're out for a walk or entertaining guests.

During the socialization process, you have to keep in mind that puppies have immature immune systems and therefore are very susceptible to disease, especially before they've received all their vaccinations. This doesn't mean that you must keep your puppy locked up in the house for the first few months of his life. It just means that, when you take him outside of the house or have people over, you must take certain precautions. Numerous parasites and diseases are carried around on the bottom of our shoes, so when you come home and when people come into your home, make sure all of you take off your shoes at the door. You and your guests should always wash your hands before handling the puppy. When you're out walking your puppy, you will no doubt come across other dog owners doing the very same thing. However, you would be best to avoid the canine greeting ritual until your puppy has received all his vaccines or you have gotten the okay from your veterinarian.

Even if you don't have children, it's important for your puppy to be exposed to kids. Keep in mind that these first experiences must be positive, so you need to stay in control of the introduction. Before you let a

references, a list of services provided, and a price list. It's also important to find out if the groomer has ever worked with a mixed breed like yours before.

When bathing your dog, use only dog-specific shampoo, not one formulated for people. Even baby shampoo is too harsh.

Your dog's gait and how often he walks on hard surfaces, such as concrete, will determine how often you need to trim his nails. Hard surfaces naturally keep a dog's nails short. You'll know it's time for a nail trim when you hear your dog's nails clicking on your kitchen tile or on the sidewalk. Letting his nails grow too long can lead to orthopedic problems, because long nails prevent your dog from walking properly.

Use dog-specific nail trimmers. Nail trimming can be difficult, especially if your dog has dark nails, which prevent you from seeing the quick. The quick houses the foot's nerve and blood supply. If you cut the nail too short, you will cause some bleeding and pain. To stop the bleeding, cover the cut nail with styptic powder or flour.

Another area you should pay attention to is your dog's ears. Your dog may have adorable floppy ears, but they can house some nasty infections. A healthy dog's ear is pink and

odor-free. An infected ear is smelly and filled with a black or dark-brown wax. If you notice the odor or a waxy buildup, make an appointment with your veterinarian. Don't try to treat it at home, as it may be either a bacterial or a viral infection, which require different treatments.

To clean your dog's ears, you'll need a pet ear wash and some cotton balls. Soak a cotton ball in the ear wash, and then squeeze it so that it's damp, not saturated. Place the cotton ball in your dog's ear and carefully rub it up and down. Don't ever put a cotton ball, or anything else into your dog's ear canal. When you're finished, allow your dog to shake off any excess moisture; this will help prevent ear infections.

CARING FOR YOUR DOG'S TEETH

Good canine dental hygiene is just as important as our own dental hygiene. A buildup of plaque and tartar can lead to painful tooth decay and expensive extractions. It can also cause heart disease. Keeping your mixed breed's chompers pearly white can be as simple as feeding him a kibble-based diet. When a dog chews the hard kibble, the pieces scrape against his teeth, thus chipping away at the plaque and tartar buildup. Some companies tout the oral health benefits of their food right on the bag. If you decide to feed your dog this type of food, make sure it's nutritionally appropriate. If you don't want to change his diet, buy a small bag and use the larger kibble as treats.

There are also numerous treats on the market to promote canine oral hygiene. Rawhides and bones are the tried-and-true favorites of many dogs. But there are now products on the market that are meant specifically to clean a dog's teeth.

Perhaps the most effective way to ward off plaque and tartar buildup is to brush your dog's teeth. Dog tooth-pastes come in all kinds of yummy flavors, like chicken, beef, and peanut butter. Don't be tempted to brush your dog's teeth with tooth-paste intended for humans, though, as human brands contain many chemicals that are dangerous for dogs. Brushing your dog's teeth with a special toothpaste may seem over the top, but it's definitely effective.

You should brush your dog's teeth at least three times a week. You can use a regular toothbrush or a finger brush. Both work equally well. Don't be afraid to put your finger in your dog's mouth. This is something you should have been doing since day one anyway, in order to get him used to the idea that you sometimes need to take things away from him.

Like humans, some dogs are just prone to having problematic teeth, and, no matter what you do, plaque and tartar will build up. In these cases, a professional cleaning by your veterinarian once a year may be necessary to avoid costly and painful extractions down the road.

Pomeranians, Papillions, Pugs, and Bichons are all breeds that have a reputation for developing dental problems. However, when it comes to dogs with one or more of these breeds mixed into the equation, it's impossible to predict what their dental work will be like.

EYE CARE

If there's a discolored discharge coming from your dog's eyes, it may stem from an environmental irritant, an overactive or blocked tear duct, or conjunctivitis. There may even be something in his eye causing the irritation. No matter what the cause, don't try to clean it yourself. Instead, contact your veterinarian immediately for an appointment.

POTTY TRAINING

Housebreaking a puppy is challenging. It won't happen overnight, and it will take a lot of patience and understanding on your part, especially when he has an accident. Puppies have elimination routines. They go

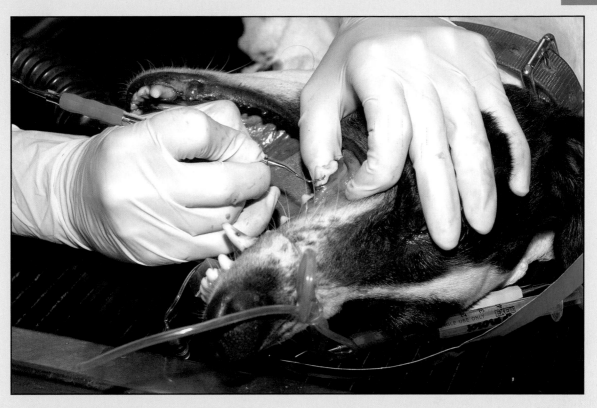

Even if you brush your dog's teeth diligently, his chompers may still require a professional cleaning each year.

when they first wake up, after they eat, following playtime, and after being confined for a long period. Knowing his routine and learning the signals that he has to go (sniffing a certain spot, standing at the door, or whining in his crate) will help you in housetraining him.

It's important to use military precision in your scheduling of meals and bathroom breaks, because this will help avoid accidents and teach your puppy to hold it as long as he physically can. For the most part, puppies ages six to 14 weeks can

hold their bladders for only an hour or two, so you'll be going outside with him eight to ten times a day. Around the 14-week mark, puppies start to gain greater control over their urges, and you'll notice a significant decrease in the number of required bathroom breaks your puppy will need each day.

At this age, he may have more control over his urinary bladder, but you cannot expect your puppy to hold it all day. He'll still need one to two midday bathroom and exercise breaks daily. If you're unable to

Housetraining a dog can be frustrating, but be patient. In time, your dog will learn that he must always do his business outside.

come home during the day, hire a professional pet sitter or ask a friend or neighbor to come by for scheduled breaks.

When teaching your puppy to eliminate outside, take him to the same location each time and use the same word(s) to encourage him, such as "Go potty," "Go pee," "Go poop," or "Do your business." When he's done, give him lots of praise.

As your puppy becomes more competent in giving you signals and not having accidents, you can increase the amount of free space you give him when you're not home. Do this slowly. If accidents occur, cut back on his free space, as it was probably too much too soon.

Accidents are going to happen; it's a fact of puppy raising. If you walk into a room and find a pile or puddle, clean it up with an enzymatic cleaner and move on. Don't punish your puppy by rubbing his nose in it or scolding him; he won't understand what he did wrong. If you catch your puppy in the act of having an accident, make a noise to get his attention, then quickly scoop him up and bring him to his designated outdoor bathroom. When he's done, praise him and clean up the accident.

HOW LONG DOES HOUSETRAINING TAKE?

On average, it will take your puppy anywhere from six months to a year or so to be completely housetrained. There is no hard and fast rule for when this should be accomplished, however. Each dog is different, no matter what his size, breed, or whether he's a purebred or a mixed-breed dog.

It will then take an additional few months of no mistakes in order for you to trust him alone in your house when you're not there. However, some dogs will move through this process more quickly or slowly than others. It all depends on your dog and how diligently you stick to your housetraining regimen.

You have to keep in mind that your puppy is not physically capable of controlling his urinary bladder for long periods, and that's not something you can speed along. No matter how long the process takes, you must remain patient and not give up. Most important, don't get angry or frustrated with your puppy when he makes mistakes. It's all part of the learning process, and he's doing the best he can.

INTRODUCING THE CRATE

Your puppy or older dog may or may not have been in a crate before you brought him home. If he's never been in one, make the introduction slowly and positively. If the toys inside the crate don't entice him to check things out, lure him into it with a treat or his meal, then quietly close the door. You don't want to slam it shut and startle the dog. Leave him in there for a few minutes then let him out. Gradually increase the amount of time you keep him in the crate so he gets the idea that this is his place.

CRATING AN ADULT DOG

If you adopt an adult dog, and he willingly goes into a crate, you can train him the same way you would a puppy. However, it's possible that the dog's previous owner misused the crate, leaving a negative impression on the dog. Depending on the severity of the dog's reaction to the crate, you may have to forgo using it, and contain your dog in a room instead.

If your adult mixed breed is a jumper and can easily hurdle over baby gates, then he'll have to be housed in the laundry room or another room with tiled flooring and a door until you're able to trust him in the house alone for hours at a time.

A puppy should never be left in his crate for more than two to four hours at a time, except overnight. Puppies can generally last a bit longer at night without needing a bathroom break. A word of caution about crates: never put a dog of any size or age into the crate with his collar on. A noise outside the house can frighten him and, depending on the severity of the fright, your dog may become stressed to the point of trying to escape from the crate. While trying to escape, his collar can get caught on some part of the crate and choke him.

MINDING HIS MANNERS

Just as we teach our children to have manners and say "Please" and "Thank you," we must also teach our dogs the value of having good manners. Good canine manners consist of not jumping all over you or your company when the dog sees you come into the house. A dog with good manners won't knock you out of the way when you both try to go through the door. Treats are taken from your hand nicely. And a well-mannered dog will readily and quickly obey any command you give him.

Training a dog requires consistency, patience, and regular practice. (For instructions on basic dog training, see pages 92–96.)

Dogs can hear sounds that we can't. By moving their ears around, much like a satellite dish, they are able to locate a sound within 6/100ths of a second.

Here's how to teach your dog good manners: every time your dog wants something from you, make him work for it by responding to a command. For example, when giving your dog a meal, tell him to sit, then put the bowl down and make him leave it. Then release him with the word "Okay," so he can enjoy his food. This is a regular reminder that you're in charge.

Making your dog do something in exchange for something he wants is not bribery. Rather, it's a great way to incorporate training into your day. This provides much-needed mental stimulation for your dog, and will go a long way toward helping him understand his place within the family. If you don't teach your dog manners, you're setting yourself up for a struggle for supremacy. Dogs have strong personalities, and when given the opportunity, they will lay claim to the top dog position in the house.

Your adopted dog may come with any of several other behavioral issues, but there is also the possibility that he might start exhibiting some bad behaviors once he makes himself at home. The reason? Most likely because he's not receiving enough exercise and structure, so he has decided to make his own fun. Chewing and barking are the most common behavioral problems for any dog.

CHEWING: If you find that your mixed breed is overwhelmed with joy when he eviscerates a plush toy or chews your shoes to shreds, this may be an indication that he's bored. In either case, you'll need to step up your game plan and provide more opportunities for your dog to engage in appropriate activities.

Dogs are social creatures, so being left alone all day goes against a dog's grain. Just because your dog has a bucket full of toys doesn't mean he's capable of amusing himself for the day. When you get home, not one toy may have been touched.

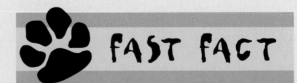

Dogs that growl while playing are typically not showing aggression, but asking other family members to come join the fun.

Make the rules and stick to them. If you don't think that you'll want your adult dog lounging on your bed or furniture, don't allow him to do these things when he's a puppy.

You may be giving your animal the wrong kind of toy. Chewers like and need chew toys.

BARKING: Barking is also a common problem for dog owners. Barking once or twice when someone knocks on the door is completely acceptable canine behavior, but if your puppy likes to bark at everybody who walks by all day long, that needs to be stopped. This behavior can be quickly curbed by not allowing him to look out the window. Let him bark once or twice, then command him into the sit or down position. By doing this, you're redirecting his attention toward something you want him to do, while directing him away from a negative behavior. If he continues to bark when people come into the house, ask your guests to ignore him; you should do this as well. Once your puppy quiets down, then you can praise him and give him attention.

One thing an owner must never do is bark back at a dog. He'll just think you're joining in the fun. You also don't want to coddle a barker verbally or physically, no matter what the circumstances. By coddling him, you're letting him know that barking is acceptable.

JUMPING ON PEOPLE: Another common behavior among many adopted dogs is jumping up on people. Probably, the previous owner had no idea how to curb this behavior. It may even have been the reason the dog was given up in the first place.

A dog will jump on people for one of two reasons: out of friendliness or out of anticipation. An anticipation jumper lunges when you have food or his favorite toy in your hand and he wants it. Like any unwanted behavior, this must be ignored in order to be stopped. If you want him to have the toy, make him sit before giving it to him. The same goes for food, providing it's intended for him.

If your dog jumps on you and every guest who comes through the door, again, ignore him. Don't look at him or touch him in any way—that includes pushing him off you. Your dog will eventually sit, look at you, and wonder what's going on. That's when you lavish him with praise and caress him.

When guests come over, they must do the same thing. To be polite, many people will say that it's okay if your dog jumps all over them—but it's not. If your dog won't stop jumping on guests, instruct them to walk away from him and ignore him until he sits. They can then go over to him and praise him.

If you have a particularly stubborn dog, you can put him on a leash and give him corrections. A leash correction, made with a flat collar, is a quick tug of the leash, accompanied by "No," immediately following your dog's negative behavior. Never, under any circumstances, knee the dog, squeeze his paws, or wrestle him to the ground in an attempt to curb his jumping. Any of these actions will actually make the behavior worse and cause the dog unnecessary pain.

URINATING: Another common misbehavior found in mixed breeds is urinating at all the wrong times. This is especially common in dogs mixed with the American Cocker Spaniel. Inappropriate urinating is usually caused by overexcitement or intimidation. Either way, it's a behavior that will eventually go away. But in the meantime, calmly and quietly clean up the accidents and go about your business.

CHAPTER SEVEN

Your Mutt Is Growing Up

Owning a mixed-breed dog is a guessing game when it comes to his growth pattern. One thing's for sure, however; during your puppy's first two years of life, he'll go through a lot of social, emotional, and, most notably, physical changes.

If your dog is a large-breed mix, he may start to seem huge by the time he's six months old. Fortunately, right when you think you're going to be living with a horse, the large-breed dog's growth slows down. He's not done growing, though. A large mixed breed's growth plates will begin to close around ten months old, but he'll continue to grow for another eight to 12 months, becoming taller and gaining more muscle mass.

By the time your dog is 18 months old, he should be close to the size he'll be as an adult.

This long growth period leaves your larger mixed breed susceptible to numerous bone and joint problems, which is why a proper diet is so important. Throughout a large mixed breed's life—but particularly before he's two years old—his diet and weight have to be carefully monitored.

Smaller mixed breeds grow until they're about 18 months of age. In general, they do not suffer from the same kinds of orthopedic issues that larger dogs often face.

KEEPING YOUR DOG HEALTHY

Your dog requires annual checkups so your veterinarian can ensure that he's in good health. The annual visit can also help stave off any serious medical conditions by catching them early. Your dog will also receive whatever annual vaccines you and your vet have decided upon when you first brought your dog into the clinic.

During the annual exam, your vet will check your dog's heart and lung function, as well as his weight, pulse, and temperature. Ears, eyes, and

VACCINATION SCHEDULE (6 MONTHS-ADULT)

The following vaccination schedule is recommended by the American Animal Hospital Association:

Vaccine	Age for Boosters
Distemper	1 year, then every 3 years
Parvovirus	1 year, then every 3 years
Parainfluenza	1 year, then every 3 years
Coronavirus	1 year, then every 3 years
Canine adenovirus-2	1 year, then every 3 years
Leptospirosis	1 year, then every 3 years
Bordetella *	1 year, then as needed
Lyme disease *	1 year, then prior to tick season
Rabies +	1 year, then every 3 years

* Optional vaccines, depending on location and risk.
+ Required by law. Some states still require annual boosters.

Source: American Animal Hospital Association

teeth are all examined for any signs of infection. The vet will also test your dog's range of motion to make sure that his limbs are not too stiff or too loose, either of which can lead to orthopedic problems down the road for large and small dogs alike.

The vet will also do an overall bump and lump check. If you have noticed any growths on your dog, be sure to point them out to the vet. The presence of lumps may indicate an infection or a tumor.

A fecal sample should be brought in to be tested for parasites, and blood will be drawn for a heartworm test. Heartworms are long, thin worms that are transmitted to dogs

THE DANGER OF HEARTWORMS

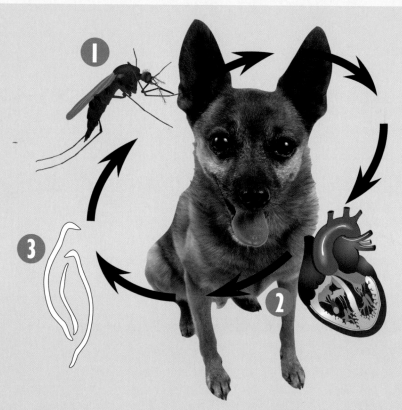

Heartworms are a concern for all dog owners. The graphic above illustrates the cycle of heartworm development. When a mosquito (1) bites a dog, it can inject microfilaria into his bloodstream. The microfilaria travel through the bloodstream to the heart (2), where they grow into heartworms (3) and multiply, clogging the dog's heart. If left untreated, heartworms can kill.

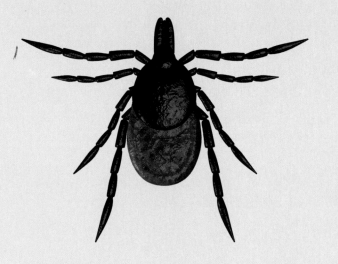

Ticks and fleas are more than just annoyances to your dog. They can carry diseases that create serious health problems for your dog.

via mosquito bites. Heartworms then travel to the dog's heart, where they multiply and can block blood vessels as well as cause breathing complications. If left untreated, heartworms can eventually bring on heart failure and death.

A dog free of parasites can be placed on a heartworm protocol, which will prevent future infestations. Whether your pooch is a lapdog or a big mix, he must be put on a heartworm preventive. Depending on the product, this may also help to fend off other parasites, such as fleas, ear mites, hookworms, and ticks.

EMERGENCIES

Any time your dog refuses to eat and doesn't want to play, you have a serious situation on your hands that must be dealt with immediately by your vet. The cause of your dog's lessened zest for life could be as simple as an upset stomach. Or it may be something that requires immediate medical attention, such as a foreign object lodged in his intestinal tract or a parasite infestation.

Downing some food off the counter may result in a bout of diarrhea or vomiting, both of which you can treat at home by not giving him any food for 12 to 24 hours. If withholding food for 24 hours seems to be working, slowly reintroduce into his diet some very bland foods, such as boiled chicken or hamburger, rice, cottage cheese, cooked pasta, or soft-boiled

FAST FACT

Dogs should never be left alone in a vehicle, especially in the summer. The car's temperature can quickly rise, causing your dog to have a heatstroke. In that case, if he's not given immediate medical attention, he could die.

eggs. If the vomiting or diarrhea returns while he's on a diet of these foods, go to the vet. If the vomiting and diarrhea has blood in it, is projected with great force, or continues for 24 hours, then you need to contact your vet immediately.

If you have an active dog, he'll no doubt get a cut or two during his life. Providing they are not deep enough to require stitches, you can clean cuts and scrapes with a sterile gauze pad and hydrogen peroxide. Once the wound site is clean, apply a topical antibiotic ointment, such as Polysporin, to help facilitate the healing process. If the cut shows signs of infection—swelling, redness, or tenderness—contact your vet.

KEEPING YOUR DOG ACTIVE

Although your mixed-breed puppy is growing up into an adult dog and slowing down a bit, you still need to give him an appropriate amount of exercise. Between six months and two years of age, on average, all dogs require a minimum of two 30-minute

WATCH FOR FOXTAILS

If you spend any amount of time hiking or camping with your mixed breed, you will have to de-foxtail your dog at some point. Foxtails are dry, grassy heads surrounded by tiny, sharp spikes, which can become lodged in your dog's fur, paws, and even in his ears, nose, and eyes. A foxtail in your mixed breed's eye can make the eye look as if it were glued shut. If the foxtails manage to get into your dog's body, they can wreak havoc by causing infections and potentially even death if they work their way into his spinal cord, lungs, heart, or brain.

Following each excursion into the wild, inspect your dog's entire body, including between the toes, for foxtails and remove them. In order to remove them, you may need to soften them up with a lubricant like mineral, vegetable, or baby oil.

Regular exercise is not just fun for your dog, it's also necessary to ensure his good health.

walks or romps in the park every day. Some of the smaller mixed breeds can thrive with less activity, but it's always a good idea to provide them with all the activity you can.

FEEDING YOUR GROWING MIXED BREED

If you have a large mixed breed, he should remain on his large-breed puppy food until he's about 12 months old, at which time you should switch him over to a food specifically formulated for large-breed adult dogs. Small and medium-sized dogs should be switched over to appropriately formulated foods at 12 months as well. Remember that any change in diet should be made gradually. Dogs can easily get sick as a result of a sudden change in brand or type of food.

Always feed your mixed breed a high-quality food to promote optimal health. Refer to the section in chapter six on puppy nutrition to review the various food options. Remember to read labels when you go to select a new brand of adult dog food as well.

SOCIALIZING A DOG

If your neighbors didn't know who you were before you got your dog, they will now. Dogs are social ambassadors. They typically want to meet everyone and everyone wants to meet them. To make all those encounters positive ones, you need to work on your dog's social etiquette as soon as he's old enough to know right from wrong.

Keep in mind that, between six months and two years of age, your dog is in the midst of his teen years. He desperately wants to please you, but he deliberately defies you. During this phase, you'll find yourself retraining him on the basic commands he once, just last week, in fact, knew so well.

TRAINING

If, for some reason, you have so far avoided puppy school or adopted a dog that never had any obedience training, then you're at a critical juncture in your relationship with your dog. He'll try to overthrow your top dog position in the family so he can claim it as his own. Obedience training can help change this.

A basic obedience class will use positive reinforcement techniques to show you how to teach your dog "sit," "down," "stay," "come," and "heel." It will also help to socialize your dog with other people and dogs. If your mixed breed has had very little training in these basic skills, it will be more difficult to teach them than it would have been when he was a 12-week-old puppy. Why? Because he's in the middle of his defiant teen years. Until now, he has not had to do as you say. Be patient. He will come around, provided you remain steadfast and consistent in instructing your dog about what you want from him. Remember, training is about teaching your dog to do what you want, when you want him to do it.

BASIC OBEDIENCE TRAINING AT HOME

You can train your dog to do just about anything you'd like, but be sure to devote some time to good manners. Basic obedience commands are considered the minimum requirements for a well-behaved dog, and they are also the foundation for any other type of training discipline you may have in mind.

If you have a smaller dog, you'll find that it's easier to communicate if you're both on the same level, rather than expecting your dog to look up at you. One way to do this is to place him on a table or higher surface; just make sure he cannot fall

Family members of all ages should get involved in training your dog.

off and get injured. You can also sit on the floor to conduct his training.

Following are some tips for teaching your mixed breed four of the most important obedience commands: sit, down, stay, and come.

SIT: Sitting is such a natural position for dogs that your dog may adopt this position on his own. If you reward him with praise or treats each time he sits, and eventually add the "sit" command, you can teach your dog to sit at your whim. If your dog can't seem to figure out what's

required, you can help him into the sit position by holding a treat above his head, just behind his eye level. When he looks up to keep his eyes on the treat, his back end may naturally drop into a sit. If not, you can further assist your dog by scooping his back legs underneath him. Plenty of repetition and generous rewards when he gets it right will have your dog sitting like an Obedience competition champ.

DOWN: You can teach your dog to lie down on command by starting from the sit position. Hold a treat on the floor in front of your dog and slowly drag it away from him. This will encourage your dog to stretch out his head and front feet as he tries to keep his nose close to the treat. If your dog stretches out even a little bit, reward him with the treat. Even if your dog has not yet reached a full down position, you should reward any movement he makes in the right direction, as many obedience skills are best taught in small increments.

The "down" command is a great way to keep your dog from getting into trouble. It can be particularly useful when you are doing something that requires your full attention, and can't afford to be distracted by your dog for a few minutes.

If your dog stands up or gets out of position, put him back into a sit and start over. A lot of patience, combined with small enough "baby steps," will eventually result in the desired behavior. Then, you can begin using the "down" command so your dog can learn to associate this word with the correct position.

STAY: The "stay" command is very useful for controlling the movement of your dog, especially in situations where safety is a concern. This command involves two components—distance and duration—that must be taught in increments. You can work on both at the same time, provided you take this training slow and don't push your dog to progress faster than he is ready.

With your dog in a sitting position, tell him, "Stay," take one step away from him, and then step toward him immediately. If your dog has maintained his sitting position, reward him. Repeat this a couple times. When your dog remains seated consistently when you take one step away, you can advance to two steps away, and so on. Gradually increase both the distance and the duration. If your dog breaks his stay at any point, it's an indication that you're expecting too much too fast. Back up a few steps and progress more slowly.

BEHAVIORAL ISSUES ASSOCIATED WITH DOGS ADOPTED FROM SHELTERS

Separation anxiety is the number-one behavioral issue faced by owners of older mixed breeds that were adopted from shelters. Who can really blame these dogs for stressing out when you leave the house, though? For all you know, the last time an owner walked out the front door, he never came back.

A stressed-out dog will chew, bark, dig at the door, have accidents in the house despite being housetrained, or pant so much that he soaks his front end with saliva. Take heed, however: separation anxiety is a treatable condition, although it requires a lot of patience and understanding on your part. If your dog has a case of separation anxiety, you'll have to be calm when you come home and find your walls chewed through or piddle puddles on the floor. Reacting to the dog's actions with anger well after the fact does nobody any good and has the potential to make the dog even more anxious.

Don't coddle your dog, either, when he starts to show his anxiousness; this will only reinforce the behavior. For example, when you're getting ready to leave for the day, don't make a big production about leaving by cuddling with your dog and saying good-bye. Just grab your stuff and go.

To help alleviate his stress, tire your dog out before leaving him alone for the day. Go for a good brisk walk, a romp in the park, or do a few minutes of basic obedience drills. A dog that has exercised his mind and body fatigues faster than one that receives no mental or physical stimulation and will enjoy a long nap when left alone.

If your dog doesn't freak out when he's contained, you may want to crate him, lock him in the laundry room, or cordon him off in another safe room with a baby gate. The den-like aspect of the crate or room may actually be soothing to him, as long as you can check on him within a few hours and let him out for a bathroom break. It's also important to leave your dog something appropriate to chew, like a food-dispensing toy stuffed with peanut butter or cookies. Giving your dog a toy when you leave accomplishes two things. One, he gets so distracted by the toy that he doesn't notice you leave; two, it gives him something to do for part of the time that he's left alone.

Depending on the severity of the separation anxiety, you may need to consult with your veterinarian about the use of medication.

The "stay" command will become a little more challenging for your dog when you are ready to practice out-of-sight stays. Your dog likes to know where you are at all times, and the minute you step out of the room, he'll attempt to follow you. Set your dog up for success by stepping out of the room for only a fraction of a second in the beginning. Return immediately to reward your dog. This way, your dog will learn that you fully intend to come back, and he'll be a little more patient in waiting for longer periods of time.

COME: The "come" command is the most important skill you can teach your dog. A dog that does not come when called is an accident waiting to happen. That's why you should practice "come" every chance you get. Keep some treats in your pocket and call your dog from different rooms in your house at different times of the day. Call your dog only once each time and reward him whenever he responds. If he doesn't come on the first call, he gets no reward.

You can practice outdoors in a fenced area or on a long leash, but again, only call your dog once each time and only reward your dog when he responds immediately. Don't force your dog to come to you by pulling on his leash, or he will quickly learn that "come" is only mandatory when he's on a leash. Instead, coax your dog to you by calling him in a happy voice or running a few steps away from him to encourage him to chase you.

The whole purpose of practicing the "come" command constantly is to condition your dog to respond automatically, without thinking about it, so that he will eventually listen to you even in the face of distractions. The command should always be presented in an upbeat manner, because if you scold or punish your dog when he doesn't come immediately, he won't be in much of a hurry to come to you the next time!

TRAVELING WITH YOUR DOG

Bringing your dog on vacation with you gives new meaning to the phrase "family vacation." To have a fun and relaxing vacation with your dog at your side, you have to do a lot of pre-planning. You'll need to research

FAST FACT

When traveling only 30 mph (48 kmph), an unrestrained 50-pound (23 kg) dog would be thrown with a force equivalent to nine 168-pound (76 kg) men, according to www.femalefirst.co.uk.

Dogs love traveling with their humans. However, when traveling by car dogs should always be strapped in or crated so they can't distract the driver and cause an accident.

your destination, route, mode of transportation, and accommodations.

With the exception of guide dogs, trains and buses don't allow dogs on board, but some airlines do. If you're going to travel by plane, you have to first find out if the airline will accept your dog. Some airlines no longer accept dogs in the passenger cabin or in the cargo hold. If you're flying to another country, find out if your canine pal will even be allowed into the country without having to be quarantined for a significant period. All of his vaccines must be up-to-

date, and you must have all necessary paperwork on hand.

When people vacation with their dogs, they typically travel by car. Driving to your destination enables you to make as many stops as necessary so your dog has ample opportunities to relieve himself and stretch his legs. Always make sure your dog is secured by a dog seatbelt, in a crate, or that he sits behind a vehicle barrier. These precautions are not only necessary to ensure your dog's safety, they let you focus on driving. Many dogs will want to sit in your lap or stand on the seat and look out the window while you're trying to drive. This should not be allowed because it may distract the driver and cause an accident.

Once you know where you're going and how you're getting there, you need to consider your accommodations. Many hotels and motels don't accept pets, so before you get in your car and decide to head out on the open road, you need to plan your overnight stays. When booking your room at a pet-friendly establishment, make sure to inquire about the hotel's pet policy. Some hotels or motels will only allow one small dog or cat in their rooms. Some won't allow any canines at all. You may also be charged an extra fee, so ask before booking the room what the fee is and whether it's refundable.

Don't forget to pack a bag for your dog. In his bag you should pack food, bowls, toys, treats, medications, and a first-aid kit. You also need to bring a blanket or bed, a collar with identification tags, a leash, and carpet cleaner because you never know if all this traveling is going to stress him out and cause him to get an upset stomach. Be sure to pack a couple of old sheets to throw over the hotel furniture in case your dog decides to make himself at home.

When planning a long trip, do research in advance to figure out where you and your dog can stay each night. Some hotels do not permit dogs on the premises, unless they are service dogs.

PET SITTERS

For some people, vacationing with their dog doesn't sound like much of a relaxing time. If you're one of them, consider some of the pet care alternatives that are available. One option is to have a friend or family member stay at your house while you're away. This causes the least amount of disruption to your dog. The person you choose for your dog should have a schedule similar to yours and be willing to do everything associated with caring for your dog, which includes feeding him at the proper times and giving him an adequate amount of regular exercise.

If you have to leave your dog at home when you travel, boarding kennels are one option. Check out potential kennels carefully and decide which one is right for your best friend. He'll get regular feeding and exercise wherever he stays, but some kennels provide more amenities than others.

If you don't know anyone who can do this, there are professional pet sitters who provide this service. Before you hire anyone, interview prospective pet sitters and pay close attention to how each one gets along with your dog. When interviewing the pet sitters, ask them for references and whether or not they are bonded and insured. It's preferable to hire a pet sitter who is bonded and insured in case anything goes awry.

Whether you have a friend, a family member, or a professional pet sitter staying at your home to care for your dog, make sure you leave the caregiver with detailed information about your dog's typical day, including his feeding schedule, which includes the amount of food he gets per meal and at what time, and where the food is located. You also need to provide information on any medication your dog is taking, including dosage and administration instructions. Also, fill in the caregiver about your dog's daily exercise requirements and where his leash is located. Tell the sitter the times he generally goes for a walk or to the park and the walking route and/or park location.

BOARDING YOUR DOG

If you don't want anyone staying at your home while you're away, you can always send your dog to a boarding facility. Many professional pet care people open their homes to other dogs. While he's there, your dog becomes a part of the family. Often, only one or two dogs are allowed at a time.

Kennels are another option. They typically house each dog in a large, no-frills room that has access to an outdoor run. There is generally minimal contact with other people and dogs, so this may not be right for dogs that require a significant amount of attention and interaction with others.

There are also 24-hour doggy day care centers. These facilities offer doggy day care during the day, which provides your mixed breed with a lot of new friends and playtime. At night, the day care center morphs into one giant bedroom where the dogs snore the night away. These types of facilities have a staff member on site to supervise the dogs throughout the night.

Prices vary for each of these services. Make sure you find out about the pickup and dropoff times and other policies, where applicable, as well as what their emergency procedures are, just in case your dog becomes injured while in their care. And you must provide them with contact information for someone other than yourself who's authorized to act on your behalf if you can't be reached in case of emergency.

CHAPTER EIGHT

Things to Do With Your Adult Dog

Participating in an activity with your dog is a great way for the two of you to forge a strong bond. Nowadays there are many activities open to mixed-breed dogs that appeal to a whole range of athletic and nonathletic tastes. No matter whether your mixed breed is large or small, it's important for him to always receive regular training, whether it's for a specific task or just to gently remind him who's the boss. For many years, there were virtually no activities a mixed breed could

An adult mixed breed will be glad to help your kids burn off some of their excess energy.

participate in because they were not recognized by the AKC and other similar organizations. Today, however, there are organizations dedicated solely to mixed breeds and their activities.

SEARCH AND RESCUE

Mixed breeds with natural scenting abilities, retrieving skills, endurance, and a desire to work alongside people make great search-and-rescue dogs. Search-and-rescue (SAR) dogs, many of which are found in local shelters and rescue organizations, are trained by the National Association for Search and Rescue to find lost or missing people who are either alive or dead. This is done in two different ways: by airborne scent or by trailing.

The SAR dog following an airborne scent tracks the person by sniffing the air. A dog trained in trailing sniffs a piece of clothing from the missing person, and then follows that specific scent wherever it leads.

SAR dogs can be specially trained for different situations, such as avalanches, disasters like hurricanes and floods, wilderness rescues, and urban searches. SAR dogs and their owners provide an invaluable service to others. It takes a lot of time and dedication to train a dog in the necessary skills, and it requires a substantial investment of time and energy to go out on a rescue. The only reward for the dogs and their owners is the chance to save a life. The dogs often become extremely

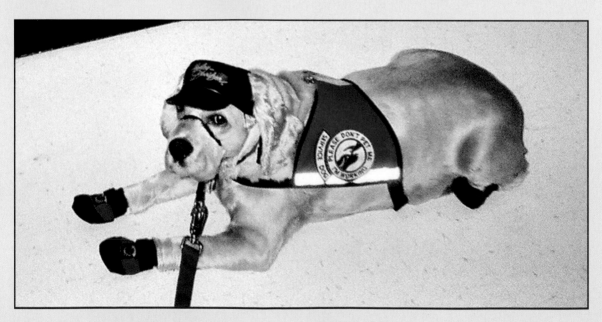

Wyatt is one of numerous mixed breeds that have found fulfilling work as a service dog.

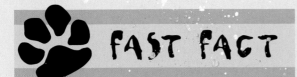

FAST FACT

Dogs trained in seizure detection alert their seizure-prone owners up to one hour before the onset of an epileptic seizure so the person can take the necessary precautions.

dedicated to finding missing people and can work themselves to exhaustion. They can also become greatly discouraged if they're unable to find people alive.

THERAPY WORK

A visit from a dog can do wonders for the spirit and recovery of a person lying in a hospital bed. Therapy dogs provide companionship and comfort to people in hospitals, nursing homes, and rehabilitation facilities. Something as simple as petting a dog can lower a person's blood pressure and help a withdrawn patient become more outgoing and engaged in the world around her.

FAST FACT

Guide dogs trained by the German government were first used after the First World War to assist blind war veterans.

therapy dog must be friendly and well mannered, which means he must be happy to meet new people and to be petted by strangers. Therapy dogs must also be able to handle crowds and be comfortable around wheelchairs, walkers, and people on crutches. Knowing a trick or two, like "Paw" or "Speak," doesn't hurt either.

COMPETITIVE SPIRIT

If you're more interested in competing with your dog, there are many options available. More often than not, it's the exuberant, high-energy dogs that end up being brought to the shelters. While these dogs may be too much to handle for some people, those who are interested in participating in canine athletics may find that these dogs are their perfect match.

The most popular sports for mixed breeds—especially those with some Border Collie in them—are Agility and Flyball.

AGILITY

Agility has become one of the most popular dog sports in North America, especially for mixed breeds. Why? Because it's a lot of fun and a great way to keep your active dog active, while at the same time reinforcing and adding new skills to his obedience repertoire.

Dogs of all sizes can compete in Agility competitions, as the jumps are adjusted for each participant's height.

Agility is an obstacle course in which your dog, along with verbal assistance from a handler, must maneuver over balance beams, run through tunnels and weave poles, and jump through tires and hoops and over bars. The dog is judged on his time and accuracy and is penalized for taking longer than the set course time, which is determined by the judges before the start of the event. Mixed breeds and AKC-registered dogs are both eligible to compete in Agility, but there are generally more mixed breeds than pure breeds competing.

Before you sign up for your first Agility class, your dog has to know the basic commands, which include "sit," "down," "stay," and "come." You should also get clearance from your veterinarian, because Agility can be hard on a dog's body. Some dogs are naturally athletic and smart, but they may not be the quickest or the best at Agility. This sport requires a great investment of time in training your dog. It cannot be done haphazardly if you expect your dog to understand what you want of him come competition day.

FLYBALL, FREESTYLE, FRISBEE, AND OTHER EVENTS

If Agility is not your dog's sport, consider Flyball or Frisbee. These sports also accept dogs from any background. Flyball is a good sport if you're interested in team competition. Frisbee is a good choice for solo outings. In addition, your mixed-breed dog can compete in events like Canine Musical Freestyle, Obedience competitions, and even certain Conformation shows.

FLYBALL: Flyball is a team relay sport with four dogs to a team. The dogs run down a track, jumping over hurdles on their way to the Flyball box. Once at the box, the dog must step on a lever that triggers the release of a tennis ball. With the ball in his mouth, the dog runs back to the starting line as fast as he can, while jumping over the hurdles

Your mixed-breed dog may not be a Frisbee competition champion, but if he's athletic he'll almost certainly enjoy catching the disc, and may learn to do it with style.

again. The first team to cross the finish line mistake-free wins. Mixed breeds with a natural retrieving ability and love of tennis balls often do well in Flyball.

Although Flyball is a great activity for exuberant and healthy dogs, it is also very hard on the canine body, especially the elbows, knees, shoulders, and hocks. That's why a lot of smaller-sized to medium-sized dogs participate in Flyball, as opposed to the larger breeds. However, that doesn't mean a bigger dog can't excel in this sport.

While this is a great physical and mental activity, you have to make sure that it's not the only physical activity your dog gets. You still need to have him participate in noncompetitive activities like walks, romps in the park, and swimming in the lake—if he likes that sort of thing.

FRISBEE: If your dog loves to retrieve Frisbees and can do it with flair, this sport is definitely for the two of you. A competition will generally consist of two parts: a freestyle portion that focuses on athleticism, presentation, and the "How cool is that" factor. The second part of the competition tests distance, accuracy, and precision.

FREESTYLE: Canine Musical Freestyle is all about showcasing the relationship you have with your dog through a routine set to music. Routines are based on your dog's obedience skills, tricks, or anything else he excels at, which is incorporated into either a Heelwork to Music routine (the dog must heel on all sides of the handler no more than four feet [1.2 m] away) or Canine Musical Freestyle routine, where

DOCK DIVING

Dock diving is quickly becoming a popular sport among many dog owners, whether they have a mixed breed or a purebred. The purpose of dock diving is to have the dog jump as far as he can. He does this by running as fast as he can along a 40-foot (12 m) dock and then jumping into a 40-foot (12 m) long pool filled with water to retrieve an object the handler has tossed in. The training for this sport is simple, especially if your dog is a natural retriever. However, the sport is not limited to retrievers and their mixes; almost any dog can succeed at dock diving.

anything goes. Freestyle competitions, which are organized by the Canine Freestyle Federation, are open to all spayed or neutered dogs, including those with health issues.

OBEDIENCE: If you want to compete in Obedience trials with your dog, be aware that mixed breeds are not allowed to participate in AKC-sanctioned events. However, organizations like the American Mixed Breed Obedience Registry and the Mixed Breed Dog Club of America have created mixed breed–only obedience competitions.

The purpose of obedience training and competition, according to the Mixed Breed Dog Club of America, is to create a smooth, strong, and happy relationship between owner and dog. Even though mixed breeds don't come from a long line of championship stock, they are still able to earn their own titles, such as the Mixed Breed Companion Dog (MB-CD), Mixed Breed Companion Dog Excellent (MB-CDX), Mixed Breed Utility Dog (MB-UD), Mixed Breed Utility Dog Excellent (MB-UDX), and Mixed Breed Obedience Trial Champion (MB-OTCh).

CONFORMATION: When mixed-breed dog owners think of Conformation

FAST FACT

Canine athletes require a special diet. In particular, they need to follow a dietary regimen that is higher in protein and fat than nonathletes need to maintain their muscle mass and keep their weight stable. But be careful to not overfeed your dog, because no matter how much he works out, he won't be able to burn off all the fat and calories.

shows, they automatically think their dogs can't compete because Conformation shows traditionally judge a dog's physical characteristics against the breed standard. Since there cannot be a mixed-breed standard, how could they compete? Mixed-breed Conformation shows judge dogs based on the fundamentals: health, personality, structural soundness, symmetry, and temperament.

CANINE GOOD CITIZEN TEST

The foundation for any canine job is the Canine Good Citizen (CGC) test. The CGC, which was implemented by the AKC in 1989, is a noncompetitive, pass-or-fail test that consists of 10 tests to determine whether a dog has great manners. (The Kennel Club of the United Kingdom has a similar program.)

While the AKC created the test, the test is open to all dogs.

The 10 tests are as follows:

ACCEPTING A FRIENDLY STRANGER:
Your dog must remain well behaved, showing no fear or shyness and not acting over-protective of his owner when a stranger approaches and shakes your hand.

SITTING POLITELY FOR PETTING:
When sitting beside you, your dog must be willing to accept being petted and touched by a stranger.

APPEARANCE AND GROOMING:
Your dog must allow a stranger to brush him, pick up each foot for examination, and check inside his ears. Your dog cannot show any signs of aggression or shyness during this process.

WALK ON A LOOSE LEASH:
Your dog must walk beside you on a loose leash while making turns and stops.

To achieve the Canine Good Citizen certification, a dog must prove that he is absolutely responsive to his handler's commands.

WALK THROUGH A CROWD: Your dog must remain calm while walking through a crowd of people. He is allowed to show interest in the people, but he cannot jump, pull, or act fearful.

SIT AND DOWN ON COMMAND, STAY IN PLACE: Your dog must follow the sit and down commands when you give them. You're allowed to give your dog the command more than once and use more than one word—a phrase is acceptable. He must then remain in the sit or down position while you walk 20 feet (6 m) away and then back.

COME WHEN CALLED: With your dog in a stay or with the evaluator distracting your dog by petting him, walk 10 feet (3 m) away from your dog, then call him to come. He must come to you.

REACTION TO ANOTHER DOG: You and your dog will walk up to another person and her dog. You will stop, shake hands, and have a quick conversation. Throughout this interaction, your dog should show no more than a passing interest in the other dog. You and your dog then walk away. Neither dog can show shyness or aggression.

REACTION TO DISTRACTION: During simulated everyday situations, your dog must remain calm. He can show a natural curiosity and be a little startled, but he cannot show aggression, panic, or fear.

SUPERVISED SEPARATION: Your dog must prove that he can be well behaved when left alone for three minutes with another person.

CHAPTER NINE

The Golden Years

Nobody likes to get older, but it's a fact of life that can't be avoided. When it comes to our canine best friends, unfortunately, dogs get older more quickly than we do. One calendar year is roughly equal to seven dog years. This means that when your dog is seven years old, he's the equivalent of a middle-aged person. This is also about the same time in your dog's life when he'll start to get a graying muzzle and have less energy. He may also experience vision and hearing loss.

Despite a drop in energy and an increased risk of developing debilitating diseases, an older dog can still be an absolute joy to be around. The crazy puppy days, the terrible twos, and the adolescent phases are long

Your senior dog may not have the energy he once did, but he'll still need daily walks.

past. They've been replaced with a confident well-mannered dog that just wants to hang out with you and enjoy life.

The best way to ensure that your adult dog remains healthy is to continue feeding him a high-quality diet, as well as providing him with an ample amount of physical and mental stimulation.

HEALTH PROBLEMS

Dogs, whether they're purebreds or mixed breeds, are defined as seniors when they're seven or eight years old. At that age, your mixed breed's annual exam with the veterinarian should also include a geriatric screening test, which will establish a baseline for later comparison. It will consist of a myriad of tests to determine the status of your dog's organ function, as well as check your dog's dental work, eyesight, joint mobility, and weight. Depending on the health of your senior mixed breed, your veterinarian may recommend increasing the frequency of his regular visits from once a year to every six months.

Age-related health issues are inevitable, despite your best efforts to prevent them. Aging mixed breeds area at risk of many conditions, including arthritis, diabetes, cognitive dysfunction syndrome, hearing and

FAST FACT

Dogs, like people, age differently. Some mixed-breed dogs will show signs of aging at a relatively young age, while others will keep acting like puppies until they're 12 or 15 years old.

vision loss, hypothyroidism, laryngeal paralysis, and kidney disease. Depending on your mixed breed's genetic makeup, he may start to suffer from some breed-specific ailments as well, such as hip dysplasia.

ARTHRITIS: Arthritis is a degenerative joint disease that results when the cartilage that covers and protects bone joints breaks down over time. This condition is especially prevalent among larger mixed-breeds dogs, because their greater weight puts more stress on their joints. Very active dogs, which subject their joints to trauma, are also susceptible. There is no cure for arthritis, but there are many supplements and medications available to help ease the pain and slow down the progression of the disease.

As dogs get older, they naturally slow down, so you may not associate your dog's slower pace with the onset of arthritis. The symptoms to look

When it comes to providing the best quality of life for your senior dog and extending his life, you need to catch any health condition early and treat it early. That's why many veterinarians now recommend twice-yearly exams for senior dogs. Your vet may also recommend an annual blood test to make sure all your dog's body systems are functioning properly.

for include decreased activity level, a reluctance to climb stairs, an unwillingness to get into the car, stiffness when he wakes up from a nap, and swollen joints. When you try to touch him in the joint areas, they may also be tender and hot. He may even snap at you when you touch his joints because they're so painful.

The most important thing you can do to help alleviate the pain of arthritis is to manage your dog's weight. If a dog is carrying around extra weight, it puts a lot of stress on his joints, which magnifies the arthritic pain. If your dog is overweight, having him drop just a couple of pounds will go a long way toward relieving his joint pain.

Numerous medications and supplements are also available to help

relieve the pain of arthritis. Your vet may prescribe an anti-inflammatory medication for your dog. These anti-inflammatories can be very effective for most dogs, but they may have side effects, such as diarrhea and vomiting, as well as the potential to cause kidney and liver damage. If you and your veterinarian decide to give your dog anti-inflammatories for an extended period, make sure to take regular liver and kidney function tests. Never give your dog acetaminophen or ibuprofen. While these drugs may work for humans, it is easy to deliver toxic doses to canines.

You can also try giving your dog joint supplements. Supplements don't provide immediate pain relief, but they are believed to help restore joint function and reduce pain with virtually no negative side effects. The most common supplements used for arthritis are glucosamine and chondroitin. Other supplements also deemed beneficial are Ester C and MSM. Check with your vet about the appropriate dosage of these supplements.

DIABETES: Diabetes is a disease in which the body does not properly use or produce insulin. In a nondiabetic dog the pancreas will produce insulin, which regulates glucose level in the body. However, in a diabetic dog, the pancreas fails to produce a sufficient amount of insulin for his body, causing the dog's glucose levels to spike and making the dog feel very sick. Symptoms include excessive thirst and urination.

Like arthritis, diabetes is common in certain breeds. So again, depending on your mixed breed's makeup, he may or may not be susceptible to this disease. Blood and urine tests conducted by your veterinarian are required to correctly diagnose dia-betes. Unfortunately, diabetes has no known cure, but can be managed quite effectively by giving your dog daily insulin shots.

COGNITIVE DYSFUNCTION SYNDROME (CDS): As dogs get older, they tend to become forgetful, withdrawn from the family, less active, and sleepier. Your dog may even start having accidents in the house. When there is no known medical reason for these occurrences, they are simply deemed age-related

Graying around the muzzle is a common sign of aging in all dogs.

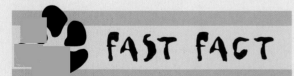

FAST FACT

Talk to your vet before concluding that your dog suffers from CDS, as some of these symptoms are also signs of adrenal gland failure, thyroid dysfunction, and kidney disease.

and dubbed CDS. There is no cure for CDS, but medications are available that may be helpful in restoring your dog's cognitive function.

HEARING AND VISION LOSS: When your mixed breed was younger, you might have thought he was deaf because he wouldn't listen to you. But as he gets older, he may actually be losing his hearing. Canine deafness is usually caused by a deterioration of the dog's inner ear. It can occur in one or both ears, and it usually results in a progressive loss of hearing.

FAST FACT

When a dog loses his hearing or vision, he may still function quite well, as his other senses will compensate somewhat for the loss.

Blindness is often the result of cataracts. Cataracts frequently affect older dogs and mixed breeds suffering from diabetes. The typical symptom of cataracts is cloudiness in the lens of the dog's eyes.

Some dogs may have cloudy eyes but not be suffering from cataracts. Instead, they might have nucleus sclerosis, which occurs as part of the natural canine aging process. When this happens, the fibers that form around the edge of the eye's lens push toward the center of the eye.

Nucleus sclerosis doesn't usually cause blindness, but it will make it difficult for your dog to focus on close-up objects. In general, dogs have great memories, despite losing their vision, so as long as you don't move or rearrange your furniture, your dog will be able to move around the house on his own quite well.

HYPOTHYROIDISM: Hypothyroidism occurs when the thyroid gland fails to produce enough of the proper hormones, causing many of the dog's organs to malfunction. Symptoms of hypothyroidism include weight gain, hair loss, dry and itchy skin, chronic ear infections, and allergies. Hypothyroidism is determined via bloodwork and can be managed with daily medication.

This older Border Collie mix is suffering from mild cataracts in both of his eyes.

LARYNGEAL PARALYSIS (LP):
Laryngeal paralysis occurs when the mixed breed's voice box (larynx) fails to open properly when the dog inhales, causing an airway obstruction. There is no known cause for the condition, but it can be the result of an injured larynx or laryngeal nerves. LP is diagnosed through a physical exam, which includes checking the dog's larynx as well as taking chest x-rays.

How would you know if your dog were suffering from LP? He'll have a difficult time breathing and will do so quite noisily. He will gag or cough when he eats or drinks. He may also have bluish-colored gums and no energy.

If your dog is diagnosed with LP, a mild case can be easily treated by adjusting some of his daily activities, such as having him avoid stressful situations, limiting his activities, especially on hot days, and keeping on eye on his weight. You may also opt to walk your dog on a harness instead of a neck collar to avoid putting more pressure on the larynx area. If he has a severe case of LP, your vet may recommend surgically removing the portion of his larynx that's creating the obstructed airflow.

KIDNEY DISEASE: Kidneys are vital to the body. They remove waste and enable the body's organs to maintain proper vitamin, mineral, and water levels. Symptoms of kidney disease include increased thirst and urination, but because these are also symptoms of other diseases, blood tests must be conducted to determine how well the kidneys are functioning. This should be part of your dog's geriatric exam.

NUTRITION FOR THE SENIOR MIXED BREED

As dogs get older, their nutritional needs change, but that doesn't mean that as soon as your dog turns seven or eight years old you need to put him on a senior diet. If you've noticed that he's packing on the pounds, you may want to either feed him less of his current adult maintenance food or switch him to a senior

It's okay to give your old pal treats, but be careful not to overdo the snack food. A dog that is 15 percent over his desirable weight is susceptible to obesity-related health problems, and this can shorten his life. Keep your pet's weight in check by watching his diet.

Swimming is excellent exercise for a senior dog, because it will not strain his hips or joints. However, when your senior dog is in the water, keep a closer eye on him than you might have when he was younger and don't let him overdo the exercise. An older dog won't have the stamina that he once did, and you don't want him to get into trouble when he tires.

food, especially if he's noticeably less active than before.

If you do decide to feed your mixed breed a food created for senior dogs, again, choose an all-natural, premium brand. The company that manufacturers the adult food you currently feed your dog may even have a senior formula. When reading the label, make sure the food is high in protein—about 25 percent. The food should also be reduced in fat and calories (when compared to an adult maintenance food) and be high in fiber.

AN OLD DOG IS STILL AN ACTIVE DOG

Your dog may have a graying muzzle and he may not be as quick as he once was, but that doesn't mean he's ready to watch the world go by from the front porch. As long as your mixed breed doesn't have any medical issues that would preclude him from continuing to enjoy his regular pursuits, he should be allowed to engage in his favorite activities. In fact, if you deny him his romps in the park and shorten his walks, you'll find that he may actually age more quickly.

SAYING GOOD-BYE

You may have spent upwards of 15 years with your dog at your side, or perhaps just a few years, but no matter how long you were together, saying good-bye will be difficult. You never want to go through the decision-making process of ending your dog's life, but it's very rare for a dog to die peacefully of old age in his sleep. You'll know when it's time to say good-bye: at this point in his life, he'll be in so much physical pain from a debilitating or terminal disease that he can no longer enjoy even the simplest pleasures. By prolonging the inevitable, you actually cause him to suffer even more.

It's terribly hard to make the decision to euthanize a pet, but the process is painless for the dog. The

As your senior dog is nearing the end of his life, take every opportunity possible to do things together and create new memories.

EXPLAINING A PET'S DEATH

If there are children in your family, don't sugarcoat the death of their canine companion. Be honest in explaining to them what has happened, whether the dog died after being hit by a car or he has finally succumbed to a debilitating disease, such as cancer. In the long run, it will be better for them to hear the truth.

This will probably be your children's first experience with death, so you need to be careful about the words you use to describe death. In particular, avoid using the word *sleep* when describing death to young children. Otherwise, they may develop a fear of sleeping because they don't want to die.

veterinarian will inject him with a drug that slows down his heart until it finally stops.

THE GRIEVING PROCESS

No doubt you will feel the loss of your constant companion, and it's important for you to honor these feelings. Friends and other family members who understand your bond will be there for you, so lean on them in this time of sorrow. If your mixed breed was one of a pack of dogs living in your home, you may find that the surviving dogs will go through their own grieving process. They may stop eating and drinking, or start to mope around the house. That's okay for a while; it's all part of their mourning.

Many people want to go right out and replace a dog they've lost in an effort to fill the void in their life. Hold off for a while before bringing another dog into your home, however. You need time to properly grieve and make peace with the passing of this dog before expanding your family. By bringing a new dog into your home too soon, you won't be able to form a unique and wonderful bond with the new dog. You will be too consumed with the old relationship you are actually trying to replicate.

Organizations to Contact

Agility Association of Canada
16648 Highway 48
Stouffville, ON L4A7X4
Canada
Phone: 905-473-3473
Fax: 905-473-9509
Email: alehmann@cherryhill
  arabs.on.ca
Web site: www.aac.ca

**American Animal
Hospital Association**
12575 West Bayaud Ave.
Lakewood, CO 80228
Phone: 303-986-2800
Fax: 800-252-2242
Email: info@aahanet.org
Web site: www.aahanet.org

American Kennel Club
260 Madison Ave
New York, NY 10016
Phone: 212-696-8200
Web site: www.akc.org

**American Mixed Breed
Obedience Registry**
P.O. Box 36
Springfield, WI 53176
Web site: www.ambor.us

Association of Pet Dog Trainers
150 Executive Center Drive, Box 35
Greenville, SC 29615
Phone: 1-800-738-3647
Fax: 1-864-331-0767
Email: information@apdt.com
Web site: www.apdt.com

The Canadian Kennel Club
89 Skyway Avenue, Suite 100
Etobicoke, Ontario
M9W 6R4 Canada
Phone: 416-675-5511
Fax: 416-675-6506
Email: information@ckc.ca
Web site: www.ckc.ca/en

Delta Society
875 124th Avenue NE, Suite 101
Bellevue, WA 98005
Phone: 425-226-7357
Fax: 425-679-5539
Email: info@deltasociety.org
Web site: www.deltasociety.org

**The Kennel Club
of the United Kingdom**
1-5 Clarges Street
Piccadilly
London W1J 8AB
United Kingdom

Phone: 0870 606 6750
Fax: 020 7518 1058
Web site: www.thekennelclub.org.uk

Mixed Breed Dog Club of America
13884 State Route 104
Lucasville, OH 45648-8586
Phone: 740-259-3941
Email: Libi-Lew@juno.com
Web site: www.mbdca.org

National Association of Dog Obedience Instructors
PMB 369
729 Grapevine Hwy
Hurst, TX 76054-2085
Email: corrsec2@nadoi.org
Web site: www.nadoi.org

National Association of Professional Pet Sitters
17000 Commerce Parkway, Suite C
Mt. Laurel, NJ 08054
Phone: 856-439-0324
Fax: 856-439-0525
Email: napps@ahint.com
Web site: www.petsitters.org

National Dog Registry
P.O. Box 51105
Mesa, AZ 85208
Phone: 800-NDR-DOGS
E-mail: info@nationaldogregistry.com
Web site: ww.nationaldogregistry.com

North American Dog Agility Council (NADAC)
11522 South Highway 3
Cataldo, ID 83810
Email: info@nadac.com
Web site: www.nadac.com

North American Flyball Association (NAFA)
1400 West Devon Avenue, #512
Chicago, IL 60660
Phone: 800-318-6312
Fax: same as phone
Email: flyball@flyball.org
Web site: www.flyball.org

Pet Sitters International
418 East King Street
King, NC 27021-9163
Phone: 336-983-9222
Fax: 336-983-3755
Web site: www.petsit.com

Therapy Dogs International, Inc.
88 Bartley Road
Flanders, NJ 07836
Phone: 973-252-9800
Fax: 973-252-7171
Email: tdi@gti.net
Web site: www.tdi-dog.org

UK National Pet Register
74 North Albert Street, Dept 2
Fleetwood, Lancashire
FY7 6BJ United Kingdom
Web site: www.nationalpetregister.org

Further Reading

Bonham, Margaret H. *The Complete Idiot's Guide to Designer Dogs*. New York: Alpha, 2005.

Brown, Andi. *Whole Pet Diet: Eight Weeks to Great Health for Dogs and Cats*. Berkeley, Calif.: Celestial Arts, 2006.

Eldredge, Debra, and Kim Campbell Thornton. *Everything Dog Health Book: A Complete Guide to Keeping Your Best Friend Healthy from Head to Tail*. Cincinnati: Adams Media Corp, 2005.

Fields Babineau, Miriam. *Training Your Mixed Breed*. Allenhurst, N.J.: Kennel Club Books, 2005.

Foster, Ken. *The Dogs Who Found Me: What I've Learned from Pets Who Were Left Behind*. Guilford, Conn.: The Lyons Press, 2006.

Guthrie, Sue, Dick Lane, and G. Sumner-Smith. *The Guide Dogs Book of Ultimate Dog Care*. Gloucestershire, United Kingdom: Ringpress Books, 2004.

Hodgson, Sarah. *Puppies for Dummies*, 2nd ed. Indianapolis: John Wiley and Sons, 2006.

Rutherford, Clarice and David H. Neil. *How to Raise a Puppy You Can Live With*, 4th ed. Loveland, Colo.: Alpine Blue Ribbon Books, 2005.

Szabo, Julia. *The Underdog: A Celebration of Mutts*. New York: Workman Publishing, 2005.

Internet Resources

http://dogs.suite101.com/article.cfm/identifyingmixedbreeddogs

Here you can find information on identifying your mixed breed's genetic makeup.

http://dogplay.com/GettingDog/mixed.html

This is a good resource for information regarding adopting and raising a mixed-breed dog.

www.dogpages.org.uk/breedbs.htm

This Web site includes a list of UK-based rescue organizations.

http://grreat.org/microchip.htm

Everything you want to know about microchipping your pet.

www.myspace.com/americanmuttshow

The Web site for the Great American Mutt Show, an event for mixed-breed dogs that includes a variety of competitions.

www.pamperedpuppy.com

This Web site offers cute gifts for dogs, as well as links to informative articles.

Index